Serial Killer's Soul

Serial Killer's Soul

Jeffrey Dahmer's Cell Block Confidante Reveals All

∞

By Herman Lee Martin

As told to Patricia Lorenz

Title Town

PUBLISHING

SERIAL KILLER'S SOUL

TitleTown Publishing, LLC
P.O. Box 12093 Green Bay, WI 54307-12093
920.737.8051 | titletownpublishing.com

Scripture quotations marked (TLB) are taken from THE WAY, The Living Bible, copyright ©1976. Used by permission of Tyndale House Publishers, Inc., Wheaton, IL 60189. All rights reserved.

Cover design by Mike Stromberg
Interior layout and design by Erika L. Block
Edited by Julie Rogers

PUBLISHER'S CATALOGING-IN-PUBLICATION DATA:

Martin, Herman Lee.
Serial Killer's Soul : Jeffrey Dahmer's Cell Block Confidante Reveals All
by Herman Lee Martin ; as told to Patricia Lorenz. -- 1st ed.
Green Bay, WI : TitleTown Pub., c2010.

p. ; cm.

ISBN: 978-0-9827206-1-5
1. Dahmer, Jeffrey.
2. Serial murderers--Wisconsin--Milwaukee--Biography.
3. Prisoners--Wisconsin--Biography. I. Lorenz, Patricia. II. Title.

HV6534.M65 M37 2010 2010934527
364.152/320977595--dc22 1009

Printed in the USA by Thomson-Shore
first edition ♻ printed on recycled paper
10 9 8 7 6 5 4 3 2 1

Put on all of God's armor so that you will be able to stand safe against all strategies and tricks of Satan. For we are not fighting against people made of flesh and blood, but against persons without bodies—the evil rulers of the unseen world, those mighty satanic beings and great evil princes of darkness who rule this world; and against huge numbers of wicked spirits in the spirit world. So use every piece of God's armor to resist the enemy whenever he attacks, and when it is all over, you will still be standing up. (Ephesians 6:11-13, The Living Bible*)*

CONTENTS

ACKNOWLEDGMENTS

Herman Martin, who was willing to open his life and his heart to share with others his incredible journey spent in the cell next to Jeffrey Dahmer.

Tracy Ertl, the joyful, hard-working owner of TitleTown Publishing, who had faith in this book from the first moment she heard about it.

Ellen Kozak, one of America's leading copyright attorneys who asked me to be the ghostwriter for this book in 1995 and who had faith in it for the fifteen years it sat in limbo awaiting the right publisher.

Julie Rogers, editor, whose amazing attention-to-detail work ethic has certainly helped make this book reader ready.

Jessica Engman, a talented intern at TitleTown Publishing who did follow-up interviews with Herman and thus provided insightful rewrites fifteen years after the original manuscript was written.

Erika Block, creator of the book's easy-on-the-eyes interior design.

Michael Stromberg, cover artist. As we all know it's the cover of a book that sells it.

Thank you to all who had a part in this book birthed, with considerable labor pains, over many years. I am especially grateful for having the opportunity to do the final rewrites and present a book that will hopefully encourage readers to think and explore on their own the many issues and ideas that this book presents.

Thank you to Herman for finally having the courage to go forward with his story fifteen years after the beginning.

Patricia Lorenz
June 1, 2010

INTRODUCTION

My curiosity overtook my fear. As I sat on my bed and stared at the gray wall separating us, I looked up at the vents at the top of my cell. Those vents led directly into Jeffrey Dahmer's cell. My eyes trailed down toward the metal sink attached to the wall. I compared the distance between the two and, if I stood on the sink, I figured I could get close to the vents. Close enough, maybe, so I could talk to him quietly. I wondered if he would talk back.

Curiosity or fear, which would prove stronger?

I took a deep breath and felt my palms getting sweaty. I stood up, went over to the sink, put both hands onto the sides, and hoisted myself up onto it. My heart was thudding so loudly I almost wondered if he could hear it. The pipes beneath the shiny metal of the sink creaked slightly under the new, unwanted addition of my weight. I steadied myself, leaning in toward the wall. I listened closely for just a moment, straining, to see if I could hear any sign of life from a man who took that very thing from so many others.

If I had met Jeffrey Dahmer before it all happened, before Tracy Edwards' escape and Dahmer's subsequent arrest, I probably would have fallen for Jeff's lies, too. I would have returned to his apartment in downtown Milwaukee, Wisconsin, and my fate may have been the same as the seventeen others whose lives he claimed. Granted, I wouldn't have gone there for the same reasons as the others, who mostly went for sex, drugs, alcohol, promises of money, or gay porn. That wasn't my bag. I would have gone to his apartment to steal stuff.

I learned to steal at an early age. Stealing is a behavioral addiction that has followed me my entire life, even now. Stealing, for me, is like a drug. After years of being clean and waiting for the right time to reveal my Dahmer story, I *still* failed to resist the urge to steal and landed back in prison. I had everything to look forward to and failed. I, along with many other people, always wondered if Dahmer was *human* when he could do the things he did. Perhaps Dahmer was indeed human but also had his own addiction? Dahmer's addiction was that he couldn't resist the compulsion to kill.

There's one thing to set straight from the start: to steal is one thing, to lie is another.

When the police arrested Jeffrey Dahmer in 1991, I was already in the Columbia Correctional Institution in Portage, Wisconsin. I was serving time for theft–armed robbery, to be specific. We watched Dahmer on the news religiously. Everyone around me watched his trial, the evidence, the gross details... *everything*. The inmates at Columbia and I heard it all. We were inmates, yet we were shocked. The entire city of Milwaukee was shocked on that July day in 1991. The *world* was shocked.

It was a virtual pandemic of fear. Parents worried about their children. Police worried that there would be a Dahmer wanna-be who would attempt to pick up where Jeff left off, a "copy-cat" killer. City officials argued about what to do with items taken from Dahmer's apartment: his tools, his photographs, and all his other belongings. People were angry, scared, and looking for someone to blame. The news stations couldn't get enough of the Dahmer story. Programs popped up about how parents could protect their children, problems with big cities, inner-city area crime, issues with the police, discrimination, and the problems with the legal system. When something like Dahmer happens, the world is full of blame and finger pointing.

Jeffrey Dahmer was born on May 21, 1960, to Lionel and Joyce (Flint) Dahmer. He started out like any normal kid, doing normal kid things. Somewhere around the age of five though, he ventured off the "normal kid" path and began to show an interest in bones and dead animals.

Around the age of ten, Jeff's dad gave him a chemistry set. Lionel Dahmer was an analytical chemist and possibly had aspirations that maybe Jeff wanted to become a scientist, too. Dead animals and bones could be a sign of an aspiring archaeologist or a penchant for biology. However, Jeff used the chemistry set to explore his interest in dead things further and not in anything resembling a "scientific" interest. The interest was more morbid fascination than science.

The set had various chemicals, things like formaldehyde and various acids. Jeff learned like an apt pupil how to use the formaldehyde to preserve animal remains and the acid to remove the skin from the bone. Jeff's morbid interest didn't apparently include actually torturing animals or even killing them, a typical trait of many serial killers; instead, he liked to mutilate the ones that were already dead ones.

One day he found a dead dog by the side of the road. He took the animal home, sawed off its head, and mounted the head on a stake in the woods near his house. He then gutted and skinned the carcass and nailed it to a tree in the shape of a cross.

Jeff's unusual interest in death wasn't his only difference from kids his age. He had a lonely childhood with few friends. In school, one could say he had a difficult time connecting with other students. He was the quiet, awkward kid who often found himself the target of anyone touting bully potential. At the same time in life, his parents were going through a nasty divorce and were often absent or absorbed in their own issues.

As the years went on, Jeff became angrier, sadder, and lonelier. He was a kid with bad ideas and parents too caught up in their own life traumas to help him through those dark times.

After his parents' divorce, everything in his life began a steep, downhill spiral. Jeff was eighteen when the divorce was final. His parents endlessly fought a proverbial tug-of-war surrounding custody of his younger brother. Jeff paid the price by being frequently ignored as he wasn't directly involved in the battle and, as a legal adult, wasn't a prize for his parents to quarrel over.

It was in June 1978, shortly after Jeff's high school graduation, when something snapped and he killed his first victim, seventeen-year-old Steven Hicks. Later, Jeff said it was an experiment … an experiment to see if he could really kill someone.

The biggest mistake of Steven Hicks' entire life was hitchhiking that night. Jeff saw him and opted to pick him up. Jeff must have already had his plan set in his head and Stephen was the unwitting target. Jeff talked Stephen into going back to his house. Agreeing, they went back to Jeff's empty home to drink some beer and hang out. After awhile, things took a drastic turn for the worse. Later, Jeff told everyone that he didn't want Stephen to leave and merely wanted to keep him around. What he did, however, was knock Steven unconscious with a barbell, rape him, and then use the same barbell to crush Stephen's windpipe, killing him.

Jeff dragged Stephen's lifeless body behind his house and buried him in a crawl space. A few years later, for whatever reason, he returned, cut up the body, and scattered the remains around a wooded lot near the house.

After high school, Jeff attended Ohio State University. His scholarly stint was short lived; after only a semester, he dropped out because he drank too much and never attended class. His dad, likely disappointed and frustrated, forced him to join the Army. In 1981, the Army decided they didn't want Jeff either, again because of his alcoholism. He was discharged and Jeff moved to Miami Beach, Florida, where he kept drinking.

Later that year he moved back to Ohio to live with his dad and stepmother, but his drinking problem continued. By the fall of 1981, Jeff officially started his criminal record when police arrested him and charged him with drunk and disorderly conduct.

His dad kicked him out.

In 1982, Jeff moved into the basement of his grandmother's house in West Allis, Wisconsin. While there, Jeff's drinking problem escalated and his behavior became even stranger. In 1982, police arrested him again, this time for indecent exposure. He was arrested a third time in September of 1986 on a second charge of indecent exposure for masturbating in front of two boys.

On September 15, 1987, almost eight years after murdering Stephen Hicks, Jeff met Steven Tuomi. The two hooked up at a gay bar in Milwaukee and ended the evening at a hotel. Jeff was drunk; too drunk to even remember murdering Steven. When Jeff sobered up and realized what had transpired, he left and bought a large suitcase. He returned to the hotel and stuffed Tuomi's body inside the suitcase. He went to his grandmother's house, suitcase in tow. In his grandmother's basement, Jeff took Tuomi out of the suitcase and had sex with the corpse. Eventually, he chopped Tuomi's body up and boiled the flesh from the bones. He packed the remains in trash bags and hauled them to the garbage.

No one ever found a single fragment of Tuomi's body.

Jeff killed again a month later, in October 1987. James Doxtator was a fourteen-year-old American Indian boy. Dahmer also met him outside a gay bar and convinced him to come back to his grandmother's house to pose for naked pictures. Jeff said he would give him fifty bucks and it was easy money. Jeff did take the photos but decided that wasn't the end of the bargain. He drugged James, strangled him to death, and took *more* photos.

Richard Guerrero, a twenty-five-year-old Hispanic man, was reported missing in March of 1988. What the world had yet to realize was that Guerrero was Jeff's next victim. Jeff, likely inspired by his previous success, did the same things to Richard that he had to Tuomi: killed him, had sex with the body, chopped it up, and threw out the remains. This time, however, he kept Richard's head and genitals as trophies.

Jeff's grandmother, oblivious to what was occurring in her own basement, had enough of her grandson's odd behavior. She had tolerated strange noises, awful smells, his drinking, and the young men he kept inviting back to her house. She kicked him out in the summer of 1988.

Jeff found an apartment in Milwaukee and was apparently enthralled with his newfound privacy. After living in the new apartment for only one day, Jeff met a thirteen-year-old Laotian boy named Somsack Sinthasomphone. Jeff lured the boy back to his apartment, where he drugged and sexually assaulted him. This boy, however, managed what the others had not; he escaped. Jeff was soon arrested, serving ten months in jail, receiving five years' probation, and registering as a sex offender.

He moved back into his grandmother's basement.

While living at his grandmother's home for the second time, Jeff met and killed twenty-four-year-old African American Anthony Sears in 1989.

Dahmer's murder toll was up to four with one failed attempt.

In May 1990, Jeff's grandmother finally kicked him out for good. She later swore she never knew about the men and boys he killed while he lived in her home. Jeff moved into an apartment in downtown Milwaukee–Apartment 213, at 924 North 25th Street. This apartment later became infamous after the truth of Dahmer's killing spree emerged.

Now that Jeff had an apartment to himself and the return of his privacy, he was free to do whatever he wanted. The apartment was in a poor, mostly black neighborhood. Jeff later confided that the area was ideal for killing because people there didn't like to get cops involved and cops, likewise, didn't seem to care as much if people who lived there went missing. He said that even if people saw something or thought something was out of ordinary, they often didn't call the cops. Drug dealing and prostitution were everyday facts and no one liked to put their nose in anyone else's business, fearing they'd mess up their own. Jeff felt a freedom he reveled in. He could do whatever he wanted.

His murderous nature in full swing, he killed as he pleased. He started to keep more trophy body parts from his victims: heads, skulls, genitals, hands, organs, torsos, skeletons, even entire bodies. He used acid to remove parts he didn't want to keep. His acid of choice turned the parts into a black, jelly-like sludge. The sludge was then poured down a sink or flushed down the toilet.

In June of 1990, Jeff met twenty-eight-year-old African American Edward Smith. As was his normal *modus operandi*, Jeff lured Smith back to his apartment, drugged him, and then killed him. Jeff cut off Smith's head, boiled off the flesh, and painted the skull gray to make it look like a replica of a medical student's model.

The next month he convinced twenty-seven-year-old Ricky Beeks to come to his place. Jeff also drugged him, killed him, and performed necrophiliac acts on the corpse. He chopped up the body, keeping random trophy parts.

Jeff seemed to target men in their twenties. He picked them up at bars or at the mall and brought them back to his apartment. Neighbors complained about the sounds and the smells. Jeff lied to get the neighbors to leave him alone, and his compulsion continued.

INTRODUCTION

In May of 1991, police *almost* caught Jeff shortly after he murdered Hughes. Jeff later said he got sloppy and lazy. He met a fourteen-year-old Laotian boy, Konerak Sinthasomphone, who just so happened to be the brother of Somsack Sinthasomphone, the young boy Jeff sexually assaulted a few years earlier.

He brought the boy back to his place where he drugged him, raped him, and took pictures. He decided to try a "zombie experiment" on the boy and actually drilled a hole in Konerak's head and poured acid into the hole. His motive, apparently, was a desire to have a zombie sex slave, one who would never want to leave him.

The teen, like his brother before him, escaped. He ran out into the street, drugged, naked, a hole drilled into his skull, and bleeding from the rectum. Jeff chased him. Two African-American women spotted the dazed boy stumbling on the street and it was too much. They called the police. Jeff arrived and demanded that the women stay out of it, but the women stood their ground and refused to return the boy to him.

When the police showed up, Jeff lied, saying the boy was nineteen, and that they were lovers. He said his lover was drunk, and they had gotten into a fight. Amazingly, the police believed him.

The cops didn't do a background check on Jeff and, ignoring the protests of the women, escorted Dahmer and the boy back to Jeff's apartment. The police came up to the apartment but didn't notice anything unusual except for a "bad smell." They accepted Jeff's explanation and left, not wanting to get involved with a homosexual dispute. Jeff wasn't taking any more chances. He quickly killed Konerak, dismembering the boy's body and saving his head.

The odor the officers reported smelling later turned out to be Tony Hughes's corpse, rotting in Jeff's bedroom.

The killing continued, escalating in frequency.

- June 1991   Matt Turner
- July 5, 1991   Jeremiah Weinberger
- July 12, 1991   Oliver Lacy
- July 19, 1991   Joseph Bradehoft

On July 22, 1991, a thirty-one-year-old African-American man named Tracy Edwards was to be Jeff's eighteenth victim, but Tracy escaped. Two officers saw him running toward them, waving them down with a handcuff around his wrist. He told them that he had fought with Dahmer when Dahmer had threatened him with a knife. Edwards and the officers returned to Jeff's place and, after a short struggle, arrested Jeff.

When police searched Jeff's apartment, they found the remains of eleven bodies. Body parts were scattered throughout the apartment in various stages of decomposition. Among the scattered remains, they found four severed heads, five skulls along with five complete skeletons and various remains of six other bodies. A fifty-seven-gallon vat filled with acid held three torsos. Police found drills, electric saws, a claw hammer, a hypodermic syringe, and, surprisingly, a King James Bible.

Reportedly, there was no food in Jeff's apartment, only condiments. Instead of food, the freezer held lungs, intestines, a kidney, a liver, and Oliver Lacy's heart.

Jeffrey Dahmer's killing spree had finally ended.

The now thirty-one-year-old man had committed grisly, unthinkable crimes. He was a man with a story no one had ever seen or heard before; a story, it seems, that came straight out of a horror movie.

Milwaukee is my second hometown and even though I was locked away during most of Jeff's rampage, it is still frightening to think that I could have easily been one of his victims. How simple would it have been for me to think I was playing him when, in fact, I was the one being played.

INTRODUCTION

Jeff was someone you watched on the news, heard about on the radio, read about in the newspapers, or talked about with your friends, all agreeing that he was "a crazy son of a bitch." At church the pastor delivered extra sermons to his flock on evil and Satan.

Jeff was the type of person you'd hear about and you were *glad* you didn't know him. You were especially glad you weren't his lawyer or his parent or his grandma or the family member of a victim or even his next-door neighbor who didn't think to call the cops.

Jeff was a man I never thought, not in a millions years, I would ever meet. He was someone I never *wanted* to meet. But there I was, Inmate 139891, temporarily in solitary confinement, sharing a cell wall with Inmate 177252, the infamous Jeffrey Dahmer.

People say the Lord works in mysterious ways and has a plan for all of us. I never would have guessed that God had this kind of a plan for me.

One
An Unholy Childhood

Don't be teamed with those who do not love the Lord, for what do the people of God have in common with the people of sin? How can light live with darkness? And what harmony can there be between Christ and the devil? How can a Christian be a partner with one who doesn't believe? (II Corinthians 6:14-15, TLB)

Prisoners and officials know me as Calvin Earl Martin, Inmate 139891. I used other names during my life of crime, but my *real* name is Herman Lee Martin.

According to police reports in most of my recent criminal records, I'm a five-foot-nine, two hundred twenty-pound black male. Beyond my unflattering mug shots and those basic criminal descriptions, I have light brown skin, keep my black hair short, and usually look clean cut and shaven when I go to work or church.

I want to tell this story because I hope people who read it think more about the amazing power of the Lord and forgiveness. First, I need to explain how I became Inmate 139891. Then, I want to share why I believe God has the power to save the soul of any man or woman, no matter how empty and corrupt their actions on earth.

I'm not proud of the way I've lived most of my life. It started with truancy in school, shoplifting, alcohol, and pot. As a teenager, I moved to hard drugs, burglary, armed robbery, car theft, cheating the government, running from the law, fathering three children out of wedlock, and spending years in and out of prison. It was an unholy mess of a life.

I was born in Memphis, Tennessee, on May 3, 1958, into a very poor family. My mother is Ollie Mae McGraw; my father, Thomas James Martin. I have six sisters and two brothers and we lived in various Memphis projects until

I was six or seven years old.

My father was an alcoholic who worked off and on as a general laborer, doing janitorial work or cleaning diesel trucks. Mom cleaned a jewelry store and worked as a maid in the home of the people who owned the store.

Dad lost jobs often because he was drunk so much. Since there wasn't enough money to support the family, when I was seven, the five of us living at home went to Arkansas to live with my Dad's aunt for a short time. My aunt was old and blind and raised hogs. I remember I stole candy from her and once even set fire to her front yard.

Not long after that fire, my father came back to get us and we moved to St. Louis, Missouri. At Cole Elementary School in third and fourth grade, I remember being a scaredy cat; I was even afraid of fire trucks. I avoided fights at all costs. I guess it showed because I got my lunch stolen often during those years.

At first, we lived in a tiny place on Finney Street in the central part of downtown St. Louis. There was a kitchen, living room, one bedroom, and one bath for the seven of us. By now, a few of my siblings were already living on their own. The kids all slept on the floor in the living room—no mattresses, just a blanket on the floor.

I *hated* being poor. There was never any money for school pictures and my clothes all came from Goodwill. I was embarrassed to go to school in those clothes.

My parents were always fighting and drinking. I remember watching them and thinking that I never wanted to be like them. I told myself that when I grew up, I would get out of this hellhole and wouldn't make the same mistakes.

Life was hard. The neighborhood was rough and, when I was only eight years old, I remember seeing a few stabbings near our house. Sometimes I look back and realize that I had no childhood innocence. I saw too much and knew too many bad things about the world around me.

We moved to another house on Finney Street, but this one was actually worse than the last. It had cockroaches and rats. By now, we were on welfare. I slept on the couch in the living room. I remember waking up because rats were crawling on me.

When I was in fifth or sixth grade, I got a job at Powell's Confectionary. My boss drank and whenever he got drunk, I'd sneak into the back room and steal two or three dollars out of his money box. I was afraid I'd get caught, but the idea of having that extra money made it worth the risk.

After a time, we moved to the west side of St. Louis, into an apartment not far from Forest Park. That apartment was better; at least I had a bed.

By now, I was about twelve years old. I got a job working with a guy who did home improvements. I learned a few skills, but the best part was that he paid in cash. I spent my earnings on clothes and movies almost as fast as I earned it.

Not long after that, we moved again; this time to a place on the north side of town. My folks always thought things would be better somewhere else. I enrolled in Enright Middle School.

That was about the time when my older sisters, Bessie and Peggy, started letting my brother Calvin and me light their cigarettes. Calvin was a year-and-a-half younger than I was. We spent a lot of time together and caused quite a bit of trouble.

Bessie worked as a bar maid at a tavern and she'd bring booze home for us. Once Calvin and I had a contest to see who could drink the most Sloe Gin. I had forgotten my promise to myself that I wouldn't go down the same road as my parents. I won the contest, but got really sick.

Eventually I started smoking pot with my school friends. Seven of us formed a gang and dubbed ourselves the very original title of the "guys in the hood." One guy's parents sold pot and my friend stole it from them for our own recreation.

We got together at night to drink, smoke pot, and stay out late. By the time I was thirteen or fourteen years old, I was riding around in stolen cars and snatching purses. I was caught taking a woman's purse once, was sent to a juvenile detention center for a month, and then was released on probation. That was my first real experience in a jail-like setting.

I wasn't afraid of jail. Everyone around me seemed to get caught doing something and end up arrested and put in jail. When I was released from juvenile, I felt like I had somehow earned the status of tough guy, and told all my friends about my "experience in the joint."

Another time I was busted and went to the Missouri Hills Reformatory, an institution for delinquent boys from the city of St. Louis. It was about thirty or forty miles from my home. I escaped from there after one week. I felt like a fugitive in a movie–running from the law and outsmarting those trying to keep me locked up. Nothing could hold me back.

That same night I went right back to the old gang and started back at the same routine, drinking and smoking pot again. Mom was still drinking heavily and now, we were told, she had diabetes. She wasn't happy to see me, so I left. I was a tough man, I didn't need her and I didn't look back. I didn't really have anywhere to go, so I moved in with friends. My freedom didn't last. A month later I was picked up for escaping the reform school and returned to Missouri Hills for eleven months. I was angry and frustrated, but after some time I realized the school wasn't all that bad.

During my stint there, I did something I was proud of for the first time in my life. I ran track. I came in first place in the relay races–more than once, too. I also played flute at the reformatory. Imagine tha–"Mister Tough Guy," playing a flute. I liked playing a musical instrument, creating something pretty.

We also took nature walks and helped with flood control by making sand bags and stacking them up along the river. I remember I enjoyed those kinds of things.

Friends and family visited every Sunday, but my folks only came once a month and they were usually drunk. I lived with two house parents in a house on the grounds with twenty other kids. When my parents showed up drunk, my house parents turned them away.

I graduated from grade school during those eleven months at Missouri Hills. Yet, as soon as I got out, I got in trouble again for helping steal a car. I was fifteen years old. This time it was determined that I would spend some time in the Boonville State Training School near Kansas.

After a month, I transferred to a halfway house in St. Louis. I enrolled in Lincoln High School and resumed smoking pot and drinking. This is how I spent my sixteenth year. I had no outlook. Teachers and cops would often ask me if I ever thought about my future, but I don't think I *understood* what they really meant by that question. Not a lot of teenagers do. I know I didn't. I didn't care because I was young, unafraid, and felt invincible. I didn't need responsibility or long-term commitments. I just lived from one day to the next.

By the time I was seventeen, I enrolled in a different high school because I'd been kicked out of Lincoln. During that year, I was always stoned. So stoned, in fact, that I did some shoplifting and couldn't even remember doing it. I also was cutting classes, taking acid and angel dust, and staying with friends for days and weeks at a time. I tried helping around the house when I'd stay with friends so I wouldn't have to pay rent. Most of the time, the people I stayed with were selling pot on the street and, if I'd bring them customers, they'd let me stay at their place for free. If I was lucky, they'd give me pot.

That same year, one of my old gang members and I used pistols to rob a drug house. We got one hundred dollars and an ounce of weed. A week later, my partner died after a shooting in his brother's pool hall. You'd think that would be an eye-opener, but it didn't stop me. I was too far under. There was no beginning or end in sight. I lived each day as it came. Life as a hustler was all I knew.

About that time my cousin, "Homey," came from Binghamton, New York, for a visit. He was a few years older than I was and worked in a foundry. My Mom and my aunt decided Homey would be a positive influence on my life, so my oldest brother and I moved to New York with him. I was excited about New York and couldn't wait to start a new life.

However, it wasn't much of a life. The three of us did a lot of drinking and pot smoking. My brother and I, it turned out, were bad influences on Homey.

I took a job cleaning the parking lot at Philadelphia Sales, a garment company. While there, I stole ten dresses, each worth about thirty-five dollars. I sold them on the street for fifteen to twenty dollars each. I kept the money in a box on the front seat of our car. Once when the police stopped me, they saw the box. When they saw the money, they became suspicious. We made up a story and they let us go. After that, I realized I had to avoid the cops. The cops just caused problems.

I felt like the cops were always after me. I decided to move out of Homey's place and move in with some other guys so the cops couldn't find me. Six months later, tired of looking over my shoulder all the time, I moved back to St. Louis.

Back in St. Louis I found a temporary job in a restaurant. It was good for a little while; but, once again, I started up my old habits of drinking, smoking pot, taking pharmaceutical pills like Valium. Eventually, I got back into heavy drugs like acid, cocaine, Christmas trees (a green methamphetamine produced using Drano crystals), and angel dust (PCP); I even started selling weed and angel dust. The money was great but it never lasted. I turned around and used the money to buy more drugs. I was selling drugs to fund my own habit.

I often showed up late for work because I partied all night. I didn't like work; I always wanted to be somewhere else.

My life was different than many other's, I guess. At the age of nineteen, many of my friends were already dead. For me, that was normal life. It didn't faze me enough to change my lifestyle. I believed death was just part of the life I lived. But I was tired of all the trouble, and now my girlfriend, Anita, was pregnant with my child. I was tired of St. Louis and, despite a baby on the way, I moved back to New York to live with Homey, who had a job driving a truck.

I don't know what made me think that things would be different in New York this time. They weren't. Right after I got there, I picked up right where I left off. Parties, drinking, and smoking pot consumed my life. Homey, a friend named Red, and I went to Atlantic City for a taste of the bright lights. We added gambling and prostitution to our list of things to do. I wanted a job in one of the casinos and thought I might be able to pick something up from the trip. Instead, right after we got there, we started snorting heroin.

We couldn't make it in Atlantic City, so Homey and I took the bus to California. We'd heard construction workers were in high demand and, since we'd never been out West, we were *sure* we'd find a better life. Our food and spending money for the trip came almost completely out of the pockets of other bus passengers. One person on the bus made the mistake of getting drunk. His mistake was my fortune; when I took his wallet, I found seven hundred dollars in it.

This made us a little paranoid so we got off the bus early. Our landing spot was Phoenix, Arizona.

We found a place to stay–the Swindle Tourist Home on Washington Street, renting a room for two for sixteen dollars a month. We stayed there for a couple months, hanging out at the local pool hall, until our money ran out.

I kept trying to figure out how to rob the owners of the tourist home, a black couple in their sixties. I knew they kept a big jar of quarters in their back room, so I snuck in one night and took it. There wasn't a lot of money in the jar, but there was enough that stealing it was worth the trouble, enough for some pot and dinner for a couple nights. After stealing the money, Homey and I moved in with another couple.

Not long after that, I got a job at the Hyatt Regency, assisting the maids and vacuuming. I met a Mexican girl who worked there. She got pregnant, but had a miscarriage. She was upset about it and, although I felt badly, I wasn't about to stick around much longer. I had already left my other girlfriend and baby, I didn't need to have that on me again.

Shortly after that, I met Addie. Addie was a prostitute. She was bringing in five hundred to six hundred dollars a day. As an added benefit, she had weapons, weed, and cocaine. I figured Addie could be my meal ticket for a while, so I quit my job and moved into her Phoenix apartment.

Just before I moved in with Addie, Homey and I had a big fight. He resented my lifestyle. The argument was so heated that I almost shot him with a pistol, but Addie got between us, begging me to stop. At the time I didn't care if Homey died or not–but I didn't want to hurt Addie.

Over time, Addie and I had a "thing" between us, but I didn't feel the need to commit. She was a prostitute and it seemed one-sided for me to be with only her. So, I decided I wanted to play around a bit. I started getting with other girls and tried not to let her find out.

I never did forget about the fight with Homey, what I saw as his betrayal against me. I was angry for a long time. It took me a while, but I finally cooled down and we settled our differences. I was glad then that I hadn't shot him. Plus, I thought, if I had, the cops would have gotten involved.

I think I was always looking for a new game. Gambling came next in my life. It was a thrill and a great way to earn a buck. One time while shootin' craps, I won more than $4,000. The first thing I did was buy a classic '66 Chevy Malibu for six hundred dollars. I loved that car. It was the first car I'd ever owned. I loved driving it and played my music loud with all the windows down. Cops turned their heads when I drove past.

In the meantime, I was still living with Addie. A nagging little voice in my head started to wonder: *What if Addie gets busted and goes to jail? What if she finds out that I'm messing around with other girls?* I knew that had the potential to get ugly. I got scared and moved out; I didn't need more trouble.

For the first time, I started thinking about my life and the more I thought, the worse I felt. I realized I was everything I told myself I never wanted to be. But here I was and it felt too late for me now. I was in over my head and there was no turning back. I couldn't see a way out of my lifestyle.

I had been thinking a lot about life and realized I'd been upset that the big plan Homey and I had of going to California to work construction had failed. I couldn't help but think it would have been nice if I had a job. A decent, steady job might help to keep me straight and out of trouble. Homey, on the other hand, missed New York and wanted to go back. I was beginning to feel the first inkling of burn out. Thinking about my life made me depressed but, ironically, it still didn't stop me from digging myself in further.

We, both Homey and I, wanted to leave town but didn't have enough money to get us anywhere. So, I did what I was good at—I stole all the electronic equipment from Addie's house, including the TV and stereo, plus any money I could find. Sure, I felt bad about doing that to her, but we needed the money.

That night, Homey and I drove to Houston, Texas. We stayed there for one month, sleeping in the car the whole time. Homey got a job as a mechanic's helper. I took up with a bunch of hustlers I met in a local pool hall. Before long I was helping with burglaries; I drove my car while they broke into places.

Finally, Homey and I got a room together in Texas but that lasted fewer than two weeks. We decided we didn't like Houston, so we moved to Dallas for a couple of days. From Dallas, we drove to Parkin, Arkansas, where some of Homey's family lived. We stayed there for a couple of weeks then drove back to St. Louis. I wanted to show off my car to my family, friends, and, especially to my old girlfriend Anita. During my absence, Anita had given birth to my first child, a little girl she named Daketa. She was born in 1978 when I was twenty years old.

Back then, it was more important to show off my car than to assume responsibility for my daughter. Besides, none of the guys in my crowd stayed around to help when their girlfriends gave birth to their children. Welfare checks took the place of fathers. That was just the way it was. I'm not proud of it, but raising a baby was the furthest thing from my mind. Getting high and figuring out ways to separate people from their money were more important.

While I was in St. Louis, I loaned my car to Homey so he could take my mother to visit his mother in New York. I left all my things in the car, including the electronic equipment I'd stolen from Addie. I thought Homey and my mom would be back in a few days.

When they didn't return, I called the New York police and reported the car stolen. Within a few days, the police called, saying they'd found the car and my cousin. I took the bus to New York. By then Homey was in jail. I got my car back only to discover that Homey had sold all the electronic equipment.

When Homey got out of jail, we met up and an argument erupted between us on a busy street. A city bus was coming. Homey was so angry that he tried to push me in front of it. I stumbled off the curb, but got out of the way just in time and the bus screeched to a stop.

Homey thought pushing me front of that bus was justified because I had tried to shoot him a few months earlier. I guess I wasn't rational, I wasn't thinking about that at the time. I was furious because he took my car, sold my stolen merchandise, and now he tried to kill me. But I'm supposed to let bygones be bygones? I couldn't stay there, I knew it was bound to get worse, so I left town. I drove to Syracuse, New York, and was determined I'd never see Homey again. I felt betrayed by the *one* person I thought I could count on. We were partners in crime, practically brothers. I learned a valuable lesson that day–I couldn't trust anyone.

I didn't let the thing with Homey keep me down. I needed money. I *always* needed money. Needing money meant only one thing: it was time for more scams.

At the Salvation Army's Rescue Mission, I lied about being homeless. They gave me an eighty-dollar food voucher and a second voucher to stay in a small room for free. Later the mission found me a better apartment at the Mayfair Hotel. It was great–I had a free place to live and focused my attention on getting money for drugs and booze.

One weekend, at a party, I saw a guy who was really drunk. Stealing from drunks was easy; they're natural targets. They don't know what is going on and even if they do realize you are trying to steal their money, they can't do much about it. I stole five hundred dollars from the guy's pocket. I didn't stay at the party much longer because the guy had friends and I was pretty sure they knew I stole his wallet.

That night I drove to Atlantic City to visit Red, who was now a pimp.

During the long, quiet drive, I tried to keep my mind off the bad things in my life, but it was hard. I thought about the usual things: where was I going to get my next meal, where was I going to stay, what was I going to do that night, or who was I going to meet up with when I got there. Eventually, I couldn't think about those things anymore because I had thought them all through. My mind wandered and the lonely road brought out the things I tried to keep out, the sad things.

Driving was about the only time I sat still long enough to think about the emptiness of my life. I had achieved nothing substantial. The only thing I owned was a car. My life was going nowhere. I was an addict, a thief, a father to babies I barely knew, and I was practically homeless. My life had no order; it was just one dead-end event leading to the next. I had no goals. I felt dead. Maybe I was?

Relief washed over me when I finally arrived in Atlantic City. The flurry of activity brought me back to the present. I forgot all the things I thought about during my drive and realized on simple thing: I needed money. Opportunity presented itself in the form of stealing some expensive antique rifles. I was excited because I knew the rifles would sell for a lot of money, but I was too nervous to sell them in Atlantic City.

I began to feel paranoid about *everything*. So, I drove to Philadelphia to sell the rifles. I hated that drive to Philadelphia. Not only was I thinking about my life *again,* but it was the first time driving on the interstate highway by myself and I was pretty scared. I was usually with Homey and, together, we gave each other courage. Now I was on my own; a black man, driving a Mustang loaded with stolen rifles. It felt like cops were everywhere and I had a bulls-eye painted on my car. I wished Homey was with me and wondered what he was doing. I wondered if he had gotten a new partner-in-crime yet. Even though I was mad at Homey, that drive to Philly made me miss him. He was really the only friend I had in the world.

When I arrived in Philly, I got rid of the stolen rifles as quickly as I could. I sold them, cheap, at a pawn shop. I managed to get just enough money for gas and food for a couple of days. It didn't really matter to me; I didn't stick around town long. I was tired so I decided to go back to St. Louis. At this point, St. Louis seemed to be the only place that really felt like home.

I couldn't get rid of that nagging certainty in my head. I was on the fast track going nowhere and I wasn't even twenty-one years old.

Two
Still Running from the Law

Their lives became full of every kind of wickedness and sin, of greed and hate, envy, murder, fighting, lying, bitterness, and gossip. They were backbiters, haters of God, insolent, proud braggarts, always thinking of new ways of sinning and continually being disobedient to their parents. They tried to misunderstand, broke their promises, and were heartless—without pity. They were fully aware of God's death penalty for these crimes, yet they went right ahead and did them anyway, and encouraged others to do them, too. (Romans 1:29-32, TLB)

I don't remember stepping into adulthood when I turned twenty-one on May 3, 1979. That's probably because I already thought I was an adult from the time I was twelve or thirteen. Barely a teenager, I had already done the things men I knew did: hustling and cheating others to make a living.

After I turned twenty-one, I got a job cleaning out sewers at the Metropolitan Sewer District in St. Louis. I needed more money to support my drug habit than the job paid, so I went to East St. Louis, on the Illinois side of the Mississippi River, and collected welfare from the state of Illinois.

That wasn't enough, so I also shoplifted on the side. I'd hit the big department stores in downtown St. Louis, like Famous Barr or Stix Baer and Fuller, and steal dozens of men's and women's suits in one day. How do you shoplift dozens of suits at a time? Easy. I'd talk to the store guard, get to know him a little, and if he seemed to be a true "brother," I'd slip him a few bucks to turn his head or go to the back of the store. I'd literally just walk out with the merchandise over my arm, pretending I was a sales rep.

That was a busy time in my life: working, shopping, hustling, shoplifting, doing drugs. It took its toll on my body and I ended up sick. I blacked out in my car one night and ended up in the hospital with pneumonia. Doctors said I almost died.

Still Running from the Law

After I got out of the hospital, I met up with Homey. It had been awhile since we'd seen each other and, despite our differences, I missed hanging with him. My close call with death–the pneumonia, not the time he tried to kill me– made me feel bad about the past and I wanted to make things right. The moment I saw him I started talking about our last big fight. Homey told me not to worry about it. He said everything was in the past and he was glad to have me back in the game.

We picked up right where we left off. One day Homey and I stole thirty or forty suits from one of the big department stores in St. Louis and took them to Milwaukee to sell.

I liked Milwaukee. Lake Michigan was beautiful and it was easy to meet people in the bars. We partied a lot at a club on Locust Street, not too far from the downtown police department. I knew the risks but I didn't care. For the moment, I finally felt like I was on top of the world; nothing could keep me down. I shrugged off all my troubles and worries.

Hustlers like me don't stay in one place for long by nature. So a few weeks later, I went back to St. Louis where I stayed with my friend "Road Dog." I got my job back at the Metropolitan Sewer District; Homey got a job there, too.

My worry-free streak didn't last long. One night Homey's brother had a birthday party in East St. Louis. In the early-morning hours after the party, we were driving home in my car and a black brother kept coming up behind me and bumping my rear bumper with his car. He didn't bump me hard, rather, just enough to get my attention. Then he'd drive alongside my car and get real close. I couldn't figure out what he wanted and, the more the little game of his went on, the angrier I got. I finally rolled down my window and demanded to know what in the hell he was doing.

He propositioned me for oral sex.

At the time, I was carrying a .38-caliber automatic pistol. I told him to pull his car over, trying to trick him into thinking I was interested. He did. I got out of my car and immediately flashed my pistol in his face. The guy seemed legitimately scared; he should be, I was really mad. I wasn't gay and I *definitely* wasn't cool with him following me, hitting my bumper, and wasting my time. I wasn't really going to shoot him, even though I have to admit the thought crossed my mind. I threatened him and tried to make him think I was serious about killing him, but then I saw a bag sitting on the back seat of his car. Seeing an opportunity, I snatched the bag and told him to get lost.

I threw the bag in the front seat of my car and drove off. When I opened the bag later, I found a couple of guns and a badge. I had just waved a gun at and robbed a Mobile Reserve Unit officer! I figured–or at least hoped–he was off duty and a homosexual just looking for some fun. But now I had his guns and badge. It didn't seem fair. I was just minding my own business. He was the one causing trouble.

I drove to Anita's house to spend the night and she met me at the door. I asked her to let me in and she adamantly refused. "You can't come in here. The police were just here looking for you," she hissed.

So I did what came naturally, I stayed with Homey for a couple days. Finally, I just left the guns in my car and took the bus back to Milwaukee. I had to get away. I was a wanted man and I couldn't go back to St. Louis. I was nervous about my warrant so, when I got to Milwaukee, I started using the name Calvin Earl Martin.

I stayed with some friends in Milwaukee, guys who were usually drunk or high. I started selling drugs and taking speed.

I needed to find more ways to make money in addition to dealing and hustling. A friend told me about welfare. In those days, it meant a free check in the mail. I didn't have to do any work so I could focus my attention on dealing. After I realized just how easy it was to get welfare in Wisconsin, I signed up under my new name. Then I used another name, "Curtis McGraw," to get a *second* monthly welfare check and food stamps. I also registered with two different addresses for the welfare checks.

About that time, I started drinking cough syrup. I was desperate, doing anything I could to get a buzz. In my head, it was the only way to escape all my troubles.

By 1981, I had a fairly profitable racket going. In addition to the two monthly welfare checks and food stamps, I stole raw materials such as copper, aluminum, brass, stainless steel, and lead from factories, foundries, and various businesses and sold my misbegotten wares to recycling companies. Some days it took me fewer than fifteen minutes to steal the stuff and, on most days, I made four hundred or five hundred dollars.

It was a pretty good chunk of money and I spent most of the it on drugs and booze. But somehow I always needed more. I went back to stealing clothing from stores. On March 18, 1982, I went to a store called the Wooden Nickel in the Capitol Court Shopping Center on the north side of Milwaukee. I paid the store guard to go in the back and turn his head. When he was clear, I robbed the store with a broken pistol. I took off and was nearly home free, but a cop chased me down.

I landed in the Milwaukee County Jail.

Going to jail that day was the new low point in my life. There I was, so strung out on drugs that I couldn't eat *and* I was facing jail time. I didn't want this life. I had no reason to live. Spontaneous and unthinking, as usual, I decided it wasn't worth it anymore and tried to commit suicide. I tore my pillowcase into strips and tied them around my neck. I wasn't even scared about doing it; I just wanted everything to be over.

In my cell, with the cloth around my neck, I tried to get as high off the ground as possible so I would have a good chance of breaking my neck. I didn't even stop to think about it or take a deep breath, I just let my whole body drop. The cloth got tight, but my neck didn't snap. I was just dangling there, slowly choking myself. Slow isn't the way it was supposed to be. I wanted it to be over, but over quickly. I tried flopping my body and jerking around, hoping my neck would break, but instead all my movement caught a guard's attention. He banged on my door and yelled something. I didn't hear him but I think he was telling me to knock it off. The guard realized I couldn't or *wouldn't* stop, so he opened my cell door and quickly cut me down. I fell to the floor and laid on my back, nearly blacking out and gasping for air.

After my vision returned, I stared at the ceiling and tried not to make eye contact with the guard.

I certainly never thanked him.

15

After my unsuccessful suicide attempt, I went to the Winnebago State Institution for "observation" for a short time. When the powers-that-be decided I was no longer a suicide risk, I was sent back to the Milwaukee County Jail, where I spent most of 1982. I was released on February 8, 1983, and received five years' probation plus a requirement to go to a Residential Drug Treatment Program in Milwaukee from February to August of 1983.

The six months I spent in that drug and alcohol rehabilitation program taught me something important: that something else was controlling my life, my addiction to drugs and alcohol.

Trouble was, the lessons I learned there didn't stay with me for long. As soon as I got out, I went right back to drugs. I couldn't help it–it was the only life I knew. For the most part, selling drugs was easy money and being high gave me a way to escape reality. Not to mention, I was still hanging out with all the same people. My old lifestyle caught right back up with me and it wasn't long before I moved in with old friends and again started hustling on the side.

My life was chaos all over again.

About that time I met Janice. We weren't together for long before she told me she was pregnant with my child. I said I was happy and promised to help out. I don't think she believed me. I don't think I believed myself, either. Janice gave birth to my baby boy.

I might have been around to help her and keep my promise, but in April 1984, I was jailed for another robbery. I managed to get out on bail. From all my run-ins with the law, I was getting good at finding ways to get around the law. When I was arrested, I used a different name, a friend's name, so they wouldn't discover I was on probation. I just happened to have a duplicate driver's license. I plea-bargained and was out of jail in thirty days. Nothing fazed me anymore. I lived a life of constant motion. I just kept moving and never looking back.

I soon met a young woman named Annie. Annie had two sons and a good job as a dispatcher with the police department. Annie was good for me at first. We moved in together and she tried to keep me straight. Keeping me straight wasn't something someone else could do though and, in 1985, I began snorting cocaine.

Still Running from the Law

I knew I had let her down.

When I needed to get away from the stress of the home, I escaped to the harness horse races at the Maywood track in Cicero, Illinois, just north of Chicago. I found my escape about four times a week. I wasn't home often and, when I was home, I was usually messed up.

One day when I was on a high, I told Annie that she wasn't good for me and I wasn't good for her. I asked her and her sons to move out. She agreed. Right after they moved out, I brought in Homey's girlfriend's sister, Barbara, to live with me. Barbara taught me how to sell *big* drugs like cocaine and heroin.

In 1986, I moved to Grand Rapids, Michigan, for a month. From there I went back to Milwaukee and discovered that someone stole my disability welfare check. I pulled a pistol on the people living downstairs from Homey and his girlfriend because I thought they stole the check. They swore they didn't; I didn't believe them.

The downstairs neighbors called the cops, who arrested me for carrying a concealed weapon. Because I was a convicted felon on parole, I was sent back to the Milwaukee County Jail, then to the Milwaukee County Psychiatric Ward, and finally to the House of Corrections in Franklin for one month. Judge Frank Crivello gave me two years' probation. I found out later that Homey and his girlfriend had actually stolen my check.

When I got out, I moved back in with Barbara. That only lasted for a week because I started back on my path of destruction. My parole officer put me in DePaul Hospital, a psychiatric hospital in Milwaukee, for rehabilitation for thirty days. Rehab gave me hope that I could change my ways. I promised myself that as soon as I got out, I would be a new man.

When I got out of DePaul, I was in a car accident and the insurance company paid me $3,000. That's a lot of money to a guy like me. I moved back in with my old girlfriend, Annie. I felt bad about letting her down before so I gave her most of the money to pay the rent, buy food, and help with her kids. It felt good. It made *me* feel good. I was happy to be helping her.

To use the cliché, old habits are hard to break. Not long after, my lifestyle began repeating itself and I found myself yet again in the House of Corrections. I stayed there from November 1986 to February 1987. After release, I landed in the DePaul/Bellevue Halfway House on the east side of Milwaukee until May 1987. No matter what I resolved to do when I was incarcerated, I just couldn't seem to keep my life under control. I was all over the place.

Annie came to visit me at the halfway house and dropped a bomb: she'd quit her job as a police dispatcher the previous year. Now, without any money coming in, her utilities had been turned off. Somehow, I felt I owed her. I really wanted to help her out. I didn't know what to do so I made a decision. I simply walked out of the halfway house.

The next month, because I had violated parole, my parole officer had me jailed. About the same time, I found out Annie was pregnant *again*. On February 16, 1988, Annie gave birth to my third child, my daughter Shan'elle.

I wanted to help Annie and the baby. I wanted to be a father and help my baby's mother. After my release, I found a job working for the company that put food in the airplanes at Mitchell Field in Milwaukee. My job was to clean out the trays that kept the food warm. I got that job under my real name, Herman Martin. Working there was really tough on me; I had co-workers who were blatantly racist. After two months, I walked out. Racism is one thing I have a hard time tolerating, and I couldn't handle it at work. Racism and intolerance aren't things a person just accepts over time. The frustration and the anger never leave, and you can't just start a fistfight with every person who says something disrespectful. I left mid-shift. Sure, I could have knocked some guy out on my way out the door or told the woman in the hall what I thought of her and her opinions just to prove a point, but it wouldn't have changed anything. I think, looking back, that I just felt tired–tired of fighting for *everything* all the time.

A few weeks later, I met a woman named Myra. Myra gets credit for being the person who turned me on to smoking cocaine. My profession, yet again, was stealing and reselling scrap materials to recycling companies. Ironically, during all this time (from 1985 to 1990), I collected Social Security checks because doctors trying to find *some* reason for why I couldn't be straight, said I was manic-depressive and schizophrenic.

Still Running from the Law

Some people might say a good hustler learns to fake all kinds of mental illnesses to get Social Security disability diagnoses. Honestly, if you aren't what society dictates you're *supposed* to be, they are usually willing to diagnose you with anything to help "explain it." Not to mention, when you're taking any drug that comes your way, it's easy to seem schizophrenic, or act like you've lost contact with reality, having hallucinations, or a split personality.

Regardless of my Social Security or my reselling scrap, my lifestyle was more than I could afford. My cocaine habit was costing me four to five hundred dollars a *day*. I was quickly coming to the end of my rope. . .

. . .I just didn't know it yet.

Once again, I went back to a hospital, this time Northwest General Hospital in Milwaukee, for a month for drug and alcohol treatment. A few days after I was finished with the treatment, I went to the Fashionation women's clothing store in Greenfield, Wisconsin, at eleven in the morning, snatched ten women's suits, and ran out the door. The clerk got my license plate and told police that I had robbed her at gunpoint, which, for the record, was not true. I don't mind taking responsibility for things I've done wrong, but I didn't even have a gun.

The cops caught me that same day and charged me with armed robbery. Because I was still on probation, I was sent to the county jail and then transferred to Dodge Correctional facility in Waupun, where I remained from August 1988 until February 14, 1989. After that, I transferred to the Milwaukee County Jail to await hearing until March 1989.

I got out on bail in March and started a home-improvement business in June. It was great while it lasted, but in February 1990, I went to trial and was found guilty for the armed-robbery charge. On February 16, 1990, Judge Laurence C. Gram Jr. sentenced me to ten years in the Wisconsin state prison system for armed robbery. Coincidentally, this same judge later sentenced Jeffrey Dahmer to sixteen consecutive life sentences.

On February 19, 1990, officials drove me to the Dodge Correctional Institution and put me in the "SMURF" unit. "SMURF" stands for Special Management Unit.

I had never experienced anything like this. I had been to *jail* countless times, but *prison* was different. Prison meant no freedom and no easy way out. My lifestyle had finally cost me everything.

Three
A New Life Begins

When someone becomes a Christian, he becomes a brand new person inside. He is not the same any more. A new life has begun! (II Corinthians 5:17, TLB)

During the ten days where I sat at the Milwaukee County Jail to await my sentencing, I met another prisoner named Levy. Meeting him changed my life.

The first day after my trial, I wasn't really in the mood for talking; honestly, who would be? I really wasn't in the mood for doing much of anything. I was depressed and, despite knowing I was responsible for all this, I felt sorry for myself. This Levy guy didn't let my lack of interest stop him from talking to me.

Levy tried to get me to open up by peppering me with questions. When I chose to answer him, which wasn't often, I answered him bluntly. I didn't feel like making friends; I wanted to be left alone. After hours of his seemingly aimless questions, he asked me if I had ever known "the goodness of the Lord." I wanted to chuckle. If I was a God-fearing man, would I really be in the place I was in? I told him I hadn't; religion was never part of my life.

Levy was the first person I'd ever met who fit the description of "filled with the spirit of God." He actually seemed to have the Lord in him, emerging from every pore in his body and every word he spoke. Levy told me about Jesus. Levy talked to me, taught me, and helped bring Jesus into my heart.

My life was never the same from that moment forward.

After Levy broke down my walls, I realized he was someone with whom I could relate. He was a black man, about my age, who had lived a hard life. He didn't talk about his past; he just talked about how the love of Jesus had saved him. I saw Levy as a mentor and a teacher. He had the peace and wisdom of an old man and whenever he talked I couldn't help but listen.

Levy was happy *all* the time. He didn't let anything bring him down. It was as if his whole being radiated . . . something. Levy loved life and he loved his Lord, and he couldn't wait to share that happiness and peace with anyone who wanted to listen or was still enough to listen. I was drawn to everything Levy told me because I wanted the same happiness I saw in him. I wanted to learn how I could be happy and finally free from all the bad things in my life.

One of the first things Levy told me was, "Prayer will change you." I wondered how, at that point, *anything* could change me. I was preparing to spend ten years in prison and, to be honest, when I looked back on my life, I didn't see much hope for a better future.

Levy wouldn't give up. He taught me everything he possibly could in those ten days. "Read the Bible," he'd say, then he'd read it with me. Sometimes he wrote down specific verses and told me to read them later, when I had more time.

Levy told me the Bible contained everything we needed to know in order to live a good life and be happy. He told me about Jesus Christ and how he died for my sins, even my armed robbery and drug abuse.

I never found out why Levy was in prison but for some reason, I assumed he was in there for life. Inmates hardly ever talked about their crimes, mostly because they don't want to think about them. No one in prison is guilty, you know? Prison is full of "innocent men," to hear them talk. Many inmates are depressed about their sentences, especially those locked away for a long time. Dwelling on your crimes and your sentence just makes you miserable.

Learning about faith from Levy helped keep my mind off bad things. He said if I just believed that the Son of God came down to this Earth and died on the cross for my sins, I, too, could gain eternal redemption. I didn't know if I could believe him. I had done a lot of bad things. Granted, I may not have been as bad as some others; but regardless, if there is a God, was he at all interested in me?

Levy reiterated that no matter how bad I'd been in the past, no matter what I'd done, God could and would forgive me. He said I could still earn a place in heaven for all eternity if I was truly sorry for the bad things I had done and believed in the goodness of God and his Son.

I was skeptical.

Levy didn't give up. The fact that I kept listening and trying to learn reflected that I wasn't giving up on myself for once either. Eventually everything Levy said started to make sense to me. Eternity sounded like a lot longer than the ten years of prison I was facing. I began to think that maybe I could serve my time in prison more productively. I started to dream dreams of getting out early for good behavior. I wanted to begin a new life on the outside, a life with God and Jesus Christ as my role models. I began to believe that having faith in Jesus was the answer, the only answer.

Levy came to me at a low point in my life. I was spinning ever faster on a downward spiral to nowhere. If it hadn't been for Levy, I would have spent my prison time thinking up new scams until I could start my life of crime and drugs all over again. Levy taught me to have faith–in God and in myself. He taught me to appreciate the goodness in all people and to see Jesus in every face.

Even though I was only with Levy for ten short days, I believe he saved my life and soul. He brought me into the company of God. He gave me a role model; he gave me a father I could love, and who would love me back unconditionally. The more I learned about the goodness of God, the more I wanted to learn.

I believed God sent Levy to me. For the first time in my life, I felt happy and whole, and knew that I was on my way to a new life and better things.

I was transferred to the Dodge Correctional Institution in Waupun, Wisconsin, on February 16, 1990. All inmates assigned to the Wisconsin prison system go to Dodge first. That's where each inmate receives a formal recommendation in terms of custody level, institution assignment, and individual program needs. Each prisoner also receives a complete physical examination by a doctor, nurse, psychiatrist, and psychologist.

Within a month, the Program Review Committee (PRC) evaluated me. They considered the crime I committed and my background, achievements (not many), as well as assessed my physical and mental well-being. They recommended the Wisconsin Resource Center in Winnebago, Wisconsin, a maximum/medium-security institution. I stayed there from March 27, 1990, until April 26, 1991.

While I was in Winnebago, I read my Bible and attended church services.

On September 16, 1990, during services in the prison chapel, Chaplain Gary Lee asked if anyone was ready to put away the life of crime and drugs and follow Christ. I thought about Levy and what he had done for me, how he'd opened up a new world, a whole new way of living. I stepped forward and said, "I'm tired of this life, Lord. I'm ready to follow you for the rest of my life."

At that moment I allowed myself to be reborn into a community of faith that serves only one master, Jesus Christ. I not only dedicated my life to God and his Son, but I also stopped using drugs.

In February 1991, I saw the PRC again and they recommended I choose where to serve the rest of my time: Dodge Correctional Institution in Waupun, the Columbia Correctional Institution in Portage, or the Green Bay Correctional Institution in Green Bay.

I prayed about the decision. Something kept nudging me to accept Columbia. I'd heard the time there wouldn't be easy, that it was a strict place. But a little voice in my head kept telling me Columbia was the right place.

I prayed specific prayers. "God, do you have a reason for me to be in Portage? You must. I feel you pushing me toward it. I'll request Columbia. I know you'll show me the reason when I arrive."

On April 26, 1991, I arrived at Columbia. Located just off Interstate 39 between Madison and Stevens Point, the Portage facility is a maximum-security prison in the Wisconsin countryside, surrounded by fields, farmhouses, and country roads. It was peaceful there, in the middle of nowhere.

Four
Another Sinner Captured

I beg you—I, a prisoner here in jail for serving the Lord—to live and act in a way worthy of those who have been chosen for such wonderful blessings as these. (Ephesians 4:1, TLB)

My temporary room was a single cell in the orientation unit at Columbia Correctional Institution, and I could leave my cell only for meals in the dayroom.

The next day, April 27, 1991, the psychologist who would ultimately decide how I spend my time at the facility interviewed me. She suggested placement on "SMURF Unit 6". After the unit manager, social worker, and psychiatrist interviewed me, Unit 7 actually became my home.

Three months later, on July 23, I was returning to the unit after recreation time when I noticed staff standing around the television, watching the news. I remembered the time: it was 2:30 p.m. Milwaukee police arrested a man for murdering a number of young men and boys.

The man's name was Jeffrey L. Dahmer.

We learned that at 11 p.m. the previous evening, cops arrested Dahmer at his Milwaukee apartment. Officers, homicide investigators, and medical examiners examined the contents of every room in his apartment and confiscated boxes, photographs, papers, freezers, plastic barrels, power tools, knives, kitchen equipment, and human body parts. As we watched the TV in the dayroom, the unit psychologist predicted that whoever this guy was, he'd end up at Columbia with us.

I went back to my cell to watch my own thirteen-inch black-and-white TV. I wanted to learn more about this man, Dahmer.

As the story unfolded, the man and his crimes became the main topic of conversation throughout the prison. No matter where we were—in the gym, in the library, outdoors, in our cells, the dayroom, classrooms, anywhere in the prison—all anyone talked about was Dahmer, speculating about the crimes and the nature of the man who committed them.

I was fixated with the case. From that day on, I watched everything I could about the gruesome murders. I read articles in the daily newspapers to keep up with the events as they unfolded. Dahmer confessed to killing seventeen men and boys and performing sex acts on them. I read all the grisly details the paper was willing to print.

Photographs and fingerprints complete, Dahmer was sent to the county jail in downtown Milwaukee. I knew that place well. The cells were small, five feet wide and eight feet long. Each contained a steel bed attached to the wall plus a stainless-steel toilet and sink and one small shelf on the wall.

Dahmer received the customary gray paper jumpsuit, his regular clothing confiscated. Prisoners were given paper so they couldn't rip their clothes up and hang themselves in their cell, like I had tried when I was jailed.

The jail itself wasn't that old, built in the early 1950s, but it sure felt and looked dated on the inside. It was in the Safety Building, which was six stories tall. Three floors were used as the jail, which held about five hundred prisoners. The rooftop was used for recreation, for jogging, or just standing around in the fresh air.

An antiquated morgue was in the basement. The basement also was used for discipline purposes for inmates who violated rules. During recent years, the jail housed prisoners from the House of Corrections in Franklin, Wisconsin, who were in Milwaukee for court hearings or trials, or for holding men with probation and parole violations.

Inmates in the county jail were often on lockdown twenty-four hours a day, seven days a week. It wasn't a pretty place. Peeling paint and graffiti covered the walls of every cell. In the winter the place was blazing hot in some places and freezing cold in others because old-fashioned radiators "heated" the jail. I remember being cold in my cell when I was there because I had no blankets or sheets, just a four-inch-thick blue mattress on top of the steel slab bed.

The only sounds were cell doors, clanging when they opened or closed, or the faint wail of police and fire sirens in the distance. That old county jail was also infested with two things I really hated: mice and cockroaches. It was the most uncomfortable place I'd ever been, so crowded that sometimes inmates slept on mattresses on the dayroom floor.

A few inmates in jail with misdemeanor offenses got jobs within the jail system. These men, called "trustees," usually do general cleaning or assist with meals. When I was there, the trustees were paid about fifteen dollars a week.

Rumor spread at Columbia that even though smoking was not allowed anywhere in the county jail, Dahmer could smoke because he was being cooperative during his confession. Dahmer had not only confessed to his crimes, he gave details including the victims' names, where he met each man or boy, how he killed them, and what he did with the bodies.

When the Columbia inmates heard that rumor, they were livid. Regardless of behavior, nobody let *us* smoke in our cells. It didn't seem fair, especially when our crimes weren't nearly as bad as Dahmer's.

We learned later that the rumors were just that–rumors; Dahmer never smoked in jail. The only time he smoked was when various court-appointed psychiatrists, psychologists, doctors, attorneys, and members of the clergy interviewed him for hours at a time. All of those interviews took place in either Judge Gram's chambers or in the library next to his chambers. Officials let Dahmer smoke during his interviews, but never in the jail itself.

Another rumor was that the guards at the county jail brought Dahmer hot *restaurant* meals after his hearings. I remembered during my stint there that, if I missed any regular meal time, all I got was a bologna sandwich and black coffee.

The truth, which I again learned later, was that the only people who brought Dahmer anything to eat from the outside were his attorney, Gerald Boyle, and Boyle's assistants. The meals they brought him were usually only sandwiches and candy.

But the gossip mill made it sound as though Dahmer was living it up in jail.

With rumors of preferential treatment running rampant, the inmates at

Columbia took an early dislike to Dahmer because they were jealous of what they thought he was getting rather than hating him because of the horrendous things he had done. Somehow, that seemed backwards. The new recreation was inventing crude jokes at Dahmer's, and his victims', expense.

"Do you know how much Dahmer's bail is? An arm and a leg."

"Do you know what kind of shampoo Dahmer uses? Head and Shoulders."

The local newspapers started providing more grisly details about Dahmer's crimes. Shocking a community of prisoners isn't an easy thing to do, honestly, but the brutality of Dahmer's crimes truly stunned us. Once again, the details of Dahmer and his crimes were the talk of the prison day after day.

Because of the publicity surrounding the case and the severe cruelty of the crimes themselves, Dahmer lived in an observation cell on the fifth floor, also known as Tier 5 East, of the county jail so he could be monitored for suicide attempts.

Tier 5 East had about one hundred and fifty single cells, each five feet wide by nine feet long. Like the rest of the prison, each cell had a sink, toilet, and a metal bunk bed.

There are seven observation cells on Tier 5 East. The observation cells are for inmates with multi-dysfunctional problems, highly publicized crimes, or prisoners needing protective custody. Dahmer, who qualified on all three counts, had a deputy posted in front of his cell twenty-four hours a day. The officer recorded all of Dahmer's daily activities and conversations in a journal.

Because most of Dahmer's victims were minorities, and because the prison population at the county jail is generally 75 percent African American, 15 percent Hispanic, and 10 percent Caucasian, the sheriff's deputies felt a distinct need to protect him from the general prison population, including known, organized gang members within the walls of the jail.

Rumors flew surrounding racial motivations in Dahmer's killings. We saw on the TV news that minority communities gathered in Milwaukee, grieving over the deaths of their young men. They were outraged to learn that merely two months before Dahmer's capture, two Milwaukee police officers returned a Laotian boy to Dahmer's apartment, and the boy died at Dahmer's hands a short time later. We even heard that one black church group went to Dahmer's apartment to perform an exorcism to "rid the place of evil."

Dahmer's actual apartment and its contents also were subject to heated debates involving different groups. Some folks wanted to auction off three hundred objects found in Dahmer's apartment to raise money for families and communities affected by his crimes. Some of the items supposedly up for auction were the refrigerator where he stored victims' body parts, hypodermic needles, vats used to remove victims' flesh from bones, and various tools he used to cut up the bodies.

The idea of an auction caused a public outcry. Some of the victims' families wanted the money from the auction because they figured they were the only ones entitled to "profit" from the tragedy. Others expressed anger, saying auctioning Dahmer's instruments of death would be blood money. The thought of people actually *wanting* these grisly items should have been part of the general outcry. Not to mention, weren't these things supposed to be evidence?

On the news, Theresa Smith, sister of victim Eddie Smith, said she wanted no part of the auction. She didn't want to receive blood money from Dahmer's belongings.

"I don't want someone saying, 'This is the axe that cut off Eddie's head,'" she said. What kind of person would want that and then *brag* about having it? Many agreed with her.

Many folks wanted all the Dahmer "memorabilia" destroyed, a necessary step to provide closure for everyone and allow them to move on from the tragedy. A group of Milwaukee businesses offered to buy the entire collection for $1 million in an attempt to stop the auction.

Everyone was angry and choosing sides. No one knew what to do and there was no good answer.

In addition to the complications of a potential auction, lawsuits were starting. The parents of the fourteen-year-old Laotian boy who died after police escorted him back to Dahmer's apartment filed a civil suit against those officers and the city of Milwaukee, citing their role in the death of their son. Other victims' families wanted to sue Dahmer for damages.

Even Dahmer's parents, Lionel and Joyce, dealt with lawsuits from people who wanted to sue them for being the original influence on Jeff's behavior. People wanted to blame something or someone for how Dahmer "turned out." They believed it *had* to be someone's fault.

Dahmer drama was everywhere, even in his prison in Milwaukee. When inmates passed Dahmer's cell on their way to the showers, they spit at him or made threats.

Every day at Columbia, we heard more stories about Dahmer at the Milwaukee County Jail. The recreational joke creation was still in full swing and more jokes filtered to our facility.

"What did Dahmer say when he was arrested at his apartment? Have a heart, guys."

"Know why Jeffrey's mother never comes over to his house for dinner? 'Cause one time she did and she told Jeff that she didn't like his friends. He said, 'Well, then just eat the vegetables!'"

Officials set Dahmer's initial court appearance, his bail hearing, for August 6, 1991. We saw on TV that he arrived at the courtroom escorted by a handful of deputies, wearing the same striped shirt and blue jeans he had on the night of his arrest. He joined his attorney, Gerald Boyle, and Boyle's assistants. The prosecuting attorneys were District Attorney E. Michael McCann and Assistant District Attorney Carol White.

Bail was set at $1 million. Even if someone did raise that kind of money, Dahmer technically couldn't be released because he had already violated his parole from 1988 surrounding the sexual assault of a thirteen-year-old Laotian boy, the brother of his later victim. Dahmer had drugged the boy, who was a high school freshman on his way home from school, and he likely would have been yet another murder victim, but the teen escaped Jeff's apartment. When the boy got home, he passed out and his parents took him to the hospital where doctors discovered he had been drugged and sexually assaulted. The boy told police he'd been at the apartment of a man named Jeffrey. Jeff was arrested and his father

30

hired Attorney Gerald Boyle to defend his son.

In January 1989, Dahmer pleaded guilty to second-degree sexual assault. In May 1989, Judge William Gardner put him on probation for five years and gave him a year in the Milwaukee County House of Correction under a work-release program. Dahmer could work during the day at his job at the Ambrosia Chocolate factory in Milwaukee but, at night, he returned to the dormitory-style corrections facility in Franklin, a suburb south of Milwaukee.

Dahmer was still on probation for that offense when the police arrested him for murder.

More rumors circulated that guards and sheriff's deputies stopped at Dahmer's cell to "look at him" or ask for his autograph. Apparently, some people thought they could make money off the autographs. This rumor proved true, but eventually the officers were reprimanded and the autograph-hounding stopped.

Dahmer was strictly protected from the general population in jail. Only when all the other inmates were in their cells would they let Dahmer out. Officers let him shower, go to the dayroom for recreation or to walk around, make a telephone call, or watch television. We heard that when Dahmer had visitors—doctors, attorneys, or family members—all other prisoners were locked in their cells.

Dahmer's preliminary hearing drew a packed courtroom. Family members, friends, and neighbors of the victims along with the throng of media filled the seats. Dahmer's father and stepmother, Lionel and Shari Dahmer, attended every day. One person missing was Jeffrey's biological mother, Joyce Flint, who lived in California. She never attended any of the hearings.

At the preliminary hearing, arraignment was set for September 10, 1991.

A fellow inmate told me and whoever else would listen that once, when talking to Dahmer in the jail, Dahmer proclaimed, "God created the world in six days. Then he made white people and that was good. Then he created black people to serve white people and that was bad." Who knows if it ever actually occurred.

During those days, Dahmer had lots of Christian literature in his cell, given to him by various ministers, priests, and nuns who came to the jail regularly to pray with the inmates or to teach Bible study.

By now, it had been almost a full year since I'd received the Lord into my life. Since then, I'd studied my Bible daily. For me, life at Columbia was pretty good. I had the right attitude. In Unit 2, Cell 35, I was active with my religion. I attended a noon Bible study in the chapel and I remember clearly how it was the first time in my life that I truly enjoyed myself, as a person. Church volunteers joined the inmates from all the units on those days at the Bible study. I looked forward to praising God and sharing my faith with others.

Pastor Gene Dawson talked to me when I was having difficulties. He's the one who encouraged me to join the Bible study group. I also attended regular classes, studying math, computers, social studies, and language. During recreation, I'd work out on the weight-lifting equipment in the gym. I stayed busy and kept out of trouble.

Every day I asked Jesus to strengthen me and give me what I needed to keep going, not just what I "wanted" but what I "needed" to be strong in my faith.

Between September 1991 and February 1992, I was determined to do my best and *be* my best in every way possible. I wasn't going to let anyone push my buttons and get me in trouble. I resolved to stay in school, do my assignments, practice my religion, attend church services and Bible study, and help other inmates.

During early February 1992, because of good behavior, I was granted a transfer to a medium-security institution of my choice. I chose to remain at Columbia.

I did a lot of reading those days. Of course, I read my Bible every day, but I also read more about Dahmer and, as I did, I found myself drawn to Bible passages about Satan. I wanted to find out more about how a man could do the things they said Dahmer did. I prayed for Dahmer, asking God to save his soul and to help him see the power of God.

Five
Trials of Life Inside Maximum Security

These wicked men, so proud and haughty, seem to think that God is dead. They wouldn't think of looking for him! Yet there is success in everything they do, and their enemies fall before them. They do not see your punishment awaiting them. They boast that neither God nor man can ever keep them down—somehow they'll find a way! Their mouths are full of profanity and lies and fraud. They are always boasting of their evil plans. They lurk in dark alleys of the city and murder passersby. Like lions they crouch silently, waiting to pounce upon the poor. Like hunters they catch their victims in their traps. The unfortunate are overwhelmed by their superior strength and fall beneath their blows. "God isn't watching," they say to themselves; "he'll never know!" (Psalms 10:4-11, TLB)

In September 1991, because of security risks, threats on his life, and the fear that he might attempt suicide, officials decided to transfer Dahmer to our facility while he awaited his trial.

Columbia Correctional Institution, a double-maximum-security facility, was a relatively new prison. Opened in June 1986, built to house four hundred and fifty male inmates but later modified for more, it averaged a little more than eight hundred prisoners. Four towers, one on each corner of the prison property, secured Columbia. Guards, armed with high-powered rifles, manned towers and patrol deputies, equipped with two-way radios, walked the perimeter of the property twenty-four hours a day, seven days a week, every day of the year. The fence around the prison was twelve feet high with coils of skin-shredding razor wire at the top. An electronically controlled sensor alerted security of any escape attempt. There has never been a successful escape from Columbia. That's the point of a double-max: to keep the bad people separated from the good.

Many inmates were on "lockdown" twenty-one hours a day, seven days a week, every day of the year. Lockdown was exactly that: locked in a cell with three hours of free time a day. Lockdown prisoners only left their cells for a half-hour for each meal and daily ninety-minute recreation, which was mostly to keep their bodies working.

When prisoners arrive at Columbia, they take a required shower and receive clean clothing—a green shirt and pants, underwear, brown socks, and brown work boots. Inmates who come from other institutions for disciplinary reasons or those with heavily publicized cases wear orange clothing.

In September 1991, word spread through the facility like wildfire that Dahmer would be living in our midst. I wasn't sure how I felt about the news. As a Christian, I made every effort to ignore other prisoners' hate-filled discussions and commentary. I had a belief that many didn't seem to share. Dahmer was, after all, another human being with a soul and I believed that he, like everyone else, had the potential for spending all eternity with God in heaven.

I wondered, because of the religious materials requests he had made, if Dahmer had asked the Lord for forgiveness or if he even understood the seriousness of his crimes.

When Dahmer entered Columbia for the first time, they stripped him of his street clothing, forced him to shower, and provided the required orange clothing. Dahmer wore orange clothing for *months* after his trial. It wasn't until the fall of 1992, when he was sent to the mental-health unit—the one we called SMURF—that he was finally allowed to wear regular prison clothes.

Dahmer moved to "Desegregation Unit 1" under heavy security. The institution administration, department staff members, the warden himself, security director, and the deputy warden accompanied him. It was a parade of officials. You'd have thought the president of the United States was visiting.

Jeff's new home was an observation cell. At Columbia, this is a "tank" made of bullet-proof glass where Dahmer could easily be monitored twenty-four hours a day, both by correctional officers positioned in a booth in front of his cell and by the two cameras inside the cell. The officers watched Dahmer for any suicide attempt and documented everything he did or said.

The glass-tank cells are the same size as regular cells but with some major differences. In the glass tank, the beds have straps attached, used to restrain prisoners to the bed, if necessary. The bed is in the center of the cell and there is no sink or toilet. The floor is a concrete slab. There's a literal hole in the concrete for the prisoner to urinate or defecate. When the prisoner finishes their "business," the guard flushes the makeshift toilet from *outside* the cell.

While inmates are in observation cells, they wear only underwear and T-shirt and are not allowed any recreation. Meals are the same as in the other units, although glass-tank prisoners can't to leave their cells to eat. Meals are served through "trap doors" in the cells and, during delivery, inmates must stand toward the rear of their cells.

During his time in the glass tank, Dahmer emerged only for showers, medical appointments, and haircuts. There's a barber chair near the officer's booth where inmates get haircuts every two weeks from barbers who visit units escorted by security officers.

Inmates *are* allowed paper and personal hygiene items. Each inmate received one razor each week for shaving but must return it after each shave. Prisoners in the glass tank can only shave while an officer observes.

Dahmer had only a mattress, paperback reading materials, and twenty-five letters a day. This seems like a lot of mail, more than someone could actually get, but after Dahmer arrived, he started getting more mail than any other prisoner. He received letters from people living across the United States and in many countries worldwide. Many people wrote simply to ask for his autograph.

From September through December, before his trial began, Dahmer received an average of five hundred letters a week. Prison rules, however, are very clear: a prisoner may only have twenty-five letters in his possession at any given time, no matter how many letters he receives.

Dahmer's "fans" and other curious correspondents sent money, various articles of jewelry, and photos of themselves. Every day the mail contained *bags* of letters for Dahmer. One day word spread that a woman sent him one hundred pairs of shoes and a watch. The shoes apparently were returned because they weren't shipped directly from the store where she bought them. The rule is that any item you receive from a retail store must bear the store's official stamp or sticker; no handwritten return address. Supposedly, he kept the watch.

Dahmer was allowed one ten-minute phone call each week. He could not smoke, have electronics (radio or TV), or have metal objects inside his cell. His meals were the same as ours. Many people on the outside who haven't experienced prison have a skewed idea of what prison food is like. Just to clear this up, it's actually quite substantial.

Breakfast was standard fare with cereal, eggs, pancakes, breads, juices, coffee, and dairy. Lunch was a main entrée, vegetable, and dessert. Supper at Columbia was another full meal also including a dessert. The food in prison always provided variety and amount of food each prisoner received was more than ample. Nobody goes hungry in prison, that's for sure. Now you know why some guys look forward to prison life . . ."three hots and a cot." Most of us eat better in prison than people outside.

While Dahmer was in the glass tank, his meals arrived on Styrofoam trays with plastic cups and utensils since he could not have metal objects in his cell.

The inmates, known as "swampers," clean the facility. I had a friend who was a swamper in the area near Dahmer's cell. He would often overhear security officers talking about our resident prison celebrity. My swamper friend said Dahmer's favorite meal was chicken and grits. He said when Dahmer was through eating chicken, the officers always searched his entire cell to make sure they got all the bones back from the chicken. They had to make sure nothing remained in his cell that could be used as a weapon or a suicide tool. A chicken bone may seem innocuous to normal people, but prisoners can be some of the most creative individuals you've ever met.

Every time Dahmer left his cell for any reason, all movement anywhere in the prison temporarily stopped. All inmates, regardless of whether they were at school or jobs, coming and going to or from visits with friends and family, or out for recreation time, were not allowed to walk in the prison hallways while Dahmer was out of his cell. Once we figured out why all movement stopped, movement that was very limited to begin with, the prisoner resentment against Dahmer grew.

On September 10, 1991, Dahmer had his arraignment in the Milwaukee

Circuit Court. With handcuffs attached to a belt and feet in shackles, he was transported to Milwaukee. During the arraignment, the judge or court magistrate explains to the accused the exact nature of the charges brought against him and explains his constitutional rights, including his right to a trial by jury.

Dahmer pleaded not guilty "by reason of mental disease or defect." A trial by jury was scheduled for January 27, 1992, before Judge Laurence C. Gram Jr. at the Milwaukee Circuit Court.

Dahmer returned to Columbia.

During the months before trial, Dahmer's family never visited him, nor did his attorney. Two of Boyle's assistants did visit for information sharing; Wendy Patrickus and Ellen Ryan discussed the proceedings. During their visits, guards handcuffed and shackled Dahmer and posted armed officers outside one of the two visiting areas used by the desegregation unit.

Various court-appointed psychologists and psychiatrists also came in waves to evaluate Dahmer. Security was such a big deal that any visits were more difficult than usual.

That fall I was living in Unit 6. One of my prisoner friends, "Shug," had a job in maintenance. One day he was outside painting the prison's window frames and screens, which included Dahmer's cell window. Shug, who is an African American, said that when Dahmer saw him at the window, he hollered, "Get away from my window, nigger."

One of the inmates painting with Shug told Dahmer, "If you weren't locked in there, you wouldn't say that."

They said that Dahmer walked away and didn't say another word. Again, whether this actually transpired or not is known only to those involved.

At the end of December, Dahmer returned to Milwaukee County Jail for his trial.

In general, the prison population wasn't sad to see him go. At least for awhile, during the trial, life returned to normal at Columbia.

Six
Life Goes on Without Dahmer

Through you I am saying to the prisoners of darkness, "Come out! I am giving you your freedom!" (Isaiah 49:9, TLB)

Some people think prison life is a dreary, boring existence where inmates sit in their cells day after day, awaiting the next meal or nightfall so they can sleep away their sentence. It's not like that at all.

Inmates at a maximum-security prison in the '90s and beyond were not "prisoners of darkness," like it says in Isaiah. Today's prisoners are, for the most part, in modern, well-organized mini-community. Various evaluations of prisoners provide information about them and great efforts are made to rehabilitate them, usually through educational opportunities.

When I first arrived at Columbia Correctional Institution in 1991, the Program Review Committee (PRC) recommended I be moved to the general population and enrolled in school. After being transfer to four different units, I ended up in Unit 2, Cell 35–a single cell on the east wing.

In September 1991, about the time Dahmer arrived at Columbia for the first time, I started school at Adult Basic Education, which provided high school education, and a computer class in Principles of the Adult Literacy System (PALS). I also learned to work on Apple computers. In addition to the three academic and computer programs I enrolled in, Columbia also offered vocational training programs where prisoners can earn a diploma from Milwaukee Area Technical College. Some of those programs include a Building Services Program, a Custodial Services Program, and a Graphics/Painting program. The theory is that, with an education and vocational training, a life on the outside is more viable.

Columbia had a library with approximately 10,000 books, including a large reference collection, Spanish language, current fiction, and many popular Western novels.

The library also had nearly thirty-five newspapers and magazines. There was a law section with current books for inmates working on their court cases.

Being in prison didn't mean you were completely cut off from society. For me, it was easy to keep up with the outside world just by reading the daily newspapers and watching TV.

During the weeks after Dahmer left for his trial, I spent much of my time reading my Bible and attending chapel services. The Wisconsin prison system provides religious services for many different religions. At our facility, there were seven services: Catholic, Protestant, Jewish, Muslim, Jehovah's Witness, Wiccan, and Native American Sweat Lodge.

That last one, the Native American Sweat Lodge, was interesting. Prison officials put up a tent outside for the Native Americans, built a fire under rocks, then poured water over the hot rocks to make the tent fill with steam; hence the name "Sweat Lodge." I never did witness the service myself, but I had some Native American acquaintances in prison who told me about it.

In addition to religious services, the prison provided weekly Bible studies held by volunteers who came to the institution from various local churches.

There were also programs and support groups, just like those you could participate in on the outside, designed to help prisoners work through some of their issues. I attended Alcoholics Anonymous and Narcotics Anonymous. Others groups included a child-molester group for those who committed sexual assault on a child, a social skills group, the Process Therapy Group for inmates suffering some sort of distress such as depression or anxiety, and an Anger Management group. The men in these groups had be an active participant. If you don't earnestly participate once you get in, the instructors don't let you come back.

In addition to those weekly meetings and other activities, some inmates had work assignments. Badger State Industries offered printing jobs for some of the men, but mostly jobs were institution work assignments including recreation or canteen assistance, maintenance, school clerk, teacher's aide, custodian, library clerk, chaplain clerk, laundry, food service, and living unit service. In the '90s, these jobs paid between eight cents and forty-seven cents an hour, depending on how the administrative staff rated the job. Usually the inmates doing these jobs had life sentences or were trustees.

Columbia offered an arts and crafts room for leisure-time activities. Many inmates went there to draw, work with leather or beads, or learn knitting or crocheting. A music room provided various instruments for those interested in playing music. Inmates could have their own instruments in the music room. There was also a gymnasium for indoor exercise or inmates went outside from May through September to run, or play tennis, horseshoes, basketball, baseball, or use the outside free weights. On special occasions during the summer, especially holidays like Memorial Day, Fourth of July, and Labor Day, they had cookouts outside.

Columbia also has a health service department with a full staff of doctors, nurses, dentists, psychologists, and psychiatrists. If inmates need medical assistance, there is always a professional there to help.

There were ten housing units at Columbia when I was there. Each unit had four tiers, two floors on the west wing and two floors on the east wing. Most units had sixty cells, some single, some double. Each cell was equipped with a metal bunk bed, desk and stool, plus a sink and toilet. The cells were eight feet wide by twelve feet long.

In addition to the regular units, there were two desegregation units, also known as solitary confinement or the "hole." I'll share more about the desegregation units later.

There was a reception/orientation unit with six single cells. Each new prisoner stayed in one of these cells while being introduced to the program, the physical plant members, and staff. Each prisoner received a ten-dollar credit to spend in the canteen until his money arrived. A prisoner's money generally came from friends and relatives, from savings he had before he went to prison or earnings from a prison job.

The length of stay on the reception/orientation unit ranged from one day to one month, depending on how long it took the staff to decide what regular unit was appropriate for the prisoner for the long term.

Within ten days of arrival, all prisoners met with the Program Review

Committee. The committee reviewed your background, achievements, and interests along with recommendations made by the assessment and evaluation committees. Finally, they assigned you to a unit and educational program.

Each housing unit at Columbia had a unit manager, a social worker, security supervisor, and unit officer staff sergeant, along with two or more security officers. Other staff members included an education representative, psychologist, health service representative, and recreation leader. Prison life today isn't what it was decades ago. Today each prison has a battalion of professionals on staff to see to prisoners' needs and safety.

Forms were available in each housing unit for inmates to fill out if they wanted an additional interview with any member of the staff. Inmates also filled out forms if they wanted medical attention, help from the librarian, or even a haircut.

We also had a form to make a telephone call. We were limited to two ten-minute telephone calls each week.

Friends and relatives could visit Columbia residents three times a week: two three-hour visits on weekdays and one two-hour visit on weekends.

Regular inmates dressed in green shirts, pants, and canvas shoes when leaving the unit to go to school, visitation, or appointments. When inmates lounged in their units or attended recreation, they could wear their own jogging suits, shorts, or T-shirts. Personal clothes had to be a solid color with no writing or pictures on the shirts, no red or black gym shoes or gang colors of any kind.

Four times a day, inmates had to stand quietly in their cells for the "count."

Meals were eaten in the dayroom, thirty-two inmates at a time. Most dayrooms had eight tables that seated four people at each table. The food was prepared before arriving at the units. Each unit had a kitchen with counter warmers to keep the food hot. The days with huge, noisy cafeterias where all inmates ate together were over. The atmosphere for meals was similar to that of a small restaurant. Of course, prisoners restricted to their cells ate their meals alone, within the confines of four small cell walls.

During recreation time, inmates could play cards, games, watch TV, or make phone calls, if approved, in the dayroom.

Saturday was cleaning day. Inmates cleaned their cells thoroughly and changed their linen. Each Wednesday, the unit laundry worker washed any of the inmates' personal clothing, with inmates furnishing detergent.

Instead of school and work assignments on Sundays, many inmates attended church and afternoon Bible study classes.

Unit 2 at Columbia housed the gang unit. It was high security with inmates ranging in age from eighteen to thirty-five. About 75 percent of the inmates were African American, 20 percent Caucasian, and 5 percent Hispanic. Inmates often came to prison, already members of a gang.

Because Dahmer's victims were minorities, he wouldn't have survived a week in Unit 2. But the rest of us . . . we survived. Truth be told, life at Columbia wasn't all that bad. If you took advantage of the education offered, the self-help programs, the Bible study classes, and the recreation, the days went by quickly.

Besides, we had a monumental trial to look forward to, thanks to the minute-by-minute media coverage surrounding anything related to the State of Wisconsin versus Jeffrey L. Dahmer.

Seven
Dahmer's Day in Court

Sigh and groan before the people, son of dust, in your bitter anguish; sigh with grief and broken heart. When they ask you why, tell them: Because of the fearsome news that God has given me. When it comes true, the boldest heart will melt with fear; all strength will disappear. Every spirit will faint; strong knees will tremble and become weak as water. And the Lord God says: Your doom is on the way; my judgments will be fulfilled! (Ezekiel 21:6-7, TLB)

Monday, January 27, 1992, was Dahmer's big day. He arrived in the courtroom wearing a brown sport coat and pants, a beige shirt, neat haircut, and glasses. To the world, he looked like a normal guy, not the monster we had envisioned him to be.

Family members, friends, and neighbors of Dahmer's victims packed the courtroom. The media and a few spectators who could squeeze in filled the rest of the seats. A special eight-foot-high, bullet-proof glass booth was installed behind the defense and prosecution tables to protect Dahmer from angry spectators. So many people were interested in seeing the trial that courthouse security readied other rooms with television hookups for spectators. Every person who entered the courtroom was searched for weapons and dogs randomly checked the courtroom itself for possible bombs or incendiary devices.

Jury selection spanned the first three days. The judge and attorneys interviewed potential jurors in the judge's chambers, away from the media and the spectators. The presiding judge was Laurence Gram Jr., from Milwaukee Circuit Court, Branch 33.

By Wednesday, attorneys selected twelve jurors and two alternates: six Caucasian men, seven Caucasian women and one African-American man. Family members of the victims were upset that the jury contained only one minority. Dahmer's victims had been mostly minorities.

When the trial began on January 30, security increased drastically in and around the courthouse. Defense Attorney Gerald Boyle described the evidence that would be presented along with testimony about the acts of necrophilia and cannibalism performed on the corpses.

District Attorney E. Michael McCann, the highest-ranking attorney in Milwaukee County government, represented the state of Wisconsin as the head prosecutor likely on the most important case in his career. That McCann handled the case himself, and not one of his assistants, demonstrated the magnitude of the case.

From the moment the trial began, it was an emotional roller coaster for the victims' families. Many cried at the reading of the charges against Dahmer and, frequently, as the trial proceeded.

Boyle tried to prove that Dahmer was mentally insane and suffered from a sexual disorder that precipitated the crimes.

McCann, conversely, tried to prove that Dahmer was sane when he drugged and killed his victims.

Boyle's lead psychiatrist in Dahmer's defense was Dr. Frederick Berlin, an expert on sexual disorders at Johns Hopkins Hospital in Baltimore. Judith Becker, a clinical psychologist and professor of Psychology and Psychiatry at the University of Arizona in Tucson, and Dr. Carl Wahlstrom, a psychiatrist from Chicago, also were experts for the defense.

Representing the prosecution was Dr. George Palermo, a well-respected forensic psychiatrist from Milwaukee, who, years earlier, had been on the staff at the Vatican; Dr. Frederick Fosdal, a psychiatrist from Madison; and Dr. Park Dietz, a criminologist and clinical professor of psychiatry and bio-behavioral sciences at the University of California-Los Angeles School of Medicine.

When Dr. Dietz interviewed Dahmer before the trial, he asked Dahmer if he would agree to videotape the interview. Dahmer didn't want him to, saying, "No, I don't want to be videotaped wearing this orange jumpsuit and I haven't shaved for so long. I'd look bad."

"How about if I get someone from the sheriff's office to shave you and we get you in some street clothes?" he asked.

Dahmer agreed. "If you can do that, fine. You can tape the interview."

Richard Heath, chief investigator for the Milwaukee County District

Attorney's office, present for all of Dahmer's interviews by the various psychiatrists, brought in three of his own shirts from which Dahmer could choose. One was light pink with a white stripe, the second was a blue stripe, and the third was a chocolate brown-and-white stripe. Dahmer chose the brown one. Later a couple of the psychiatrists revealed that people with strong sexual personalities often wear brown.

(NOTE: During an interview with author Lorenz, Heath revealed the following about that interview.)

The videotaped interview with Dr. Dietz lasted four days and encompassed twenty hours of tape. Jeff smoked the entire time, switching from Marlboros to menthol cigarettes.

"What's wrong with you?" Dietz asked Dahmer.

Dahmer paused. "I don't know. You're the doctor. I don't think it's evil spirits. . . and I'm not in a cult. You know I bought a table and made sort of a shrine. I'd put each victim on that table and then just sit back in my big leather chair and look at the body. It made me feel powerful. Sometimes I'd take photos of the bodies before and after killing them. I controlled them like the guy in *Silence of the Lambs*."

"Why do you think you got caught, Jeff?" Dr. Dietz asked.

"Simple," he replied, "I just got behind in my work, too many bodies stacking up in my apartment. I couldn't keep up."

Other witnesses during Dahmer's trial included:

- The man hired to remove blood stains on the carpet in the apartment rented by Dahmer at the Oxford Apartment building at 924 N. 25th Street in Milwaukee;

- The employee from a hardware store where Dahmer purchased the muriatic acid he used to dissolve human flesh from the bones of his victims;

- The man who sold Dahmer the large blue barrel he used as a vat to store body parts;

- The pharmacist who sold Dahmer the prescription of Halcyon, the drug he used to subdue his victims;

- The Milwaukee police officer who had contact with Dahmer for other offenses;
- Milwaukee police detectives Patrick Kennedy and Dennis Murphy, who interrogated Dahmer on July 23, 1991, the day after he was arrested, and who took his one hundred-and-sixty-page signed confession;
- Tracy Edwards, the young man who would have been Dahmer's eighteenth victim, but who was able to free himself and alert authorities on the evening of July 22, 1991, leading to Dahmer's arrest;
- Ronald Flowers, who met Dahmer at a gay bar a year or two previous to Dahmer's arrest;
- Somsack Sinthasomphone, the brother of Dahmer's youngest victim, Konerak Sinthasomphone. Dahmer sexually assaulted Somsack, a Laotian minor, in 1988. Because of this crime, Dahmer received five years' probation and one year at the work-release program in Franklin in May 1989. He was still on probation when he was arrested for the murders and, amazingly, he still saw his probation officer on a weekly basis during the entire killing spree;
- Police Lt. Scott Schaefer, who arrested Dahmer in September 1988 for the sexual assault on Somsack Sinthasomphone;
- A supervisor and a plant superintendent from the Ambrosia Chocolate factory, where Dahmer worked;
- Milwaukee police officers John Balcerzak and Joe Gabrish, who returned Konerak Sinthasomphone to Dahmer's custody in 1991 just before Dahmer killed the young Laotian boy;
- Sopa Princewell, manager of the Oxford Apartment building; and
- The manager of the Club Unicorn Bathhouse in Chicago, which Dahmer frequented ten times between April 1990 and February 1991.

And so it went, witness after witness, one gruesome tale after another.

Each day of the trial, sheriff's deputies escorted Dahmer to and from court. Every day the officers altered routes to the courthouse, fearing someone would learn where Dahmer was and try to kill him en route.

Dahmer's daily activities at the county jail during trial recess were limited to reading, eating, and sleeping.

Quite often during the trial, the victims' family members couldn't take hearing about the brutality of Dahmer's crimes and would leave the courtroom. Others were more stoic and stayed throughout the whole ordeal.

People throughout the country watched the entire trial on a "pay-per-view" basis, provided by local cable companies. People in the Milwaukee area listened daily to the trial in its entirety on WTMJ radio.

On Friday, February 14, 1992, closing arguments finished and the jury held Dahmer's fate in their hands. The question: Was Jeffrey Lionel Dahmer insane when he killed fifteen men and boys in Wisconsin?

Since Dahmer plead guilty by reason of mental disease or defect, the purpose of the trial was to simply determine if he really *was* insane when he committed the crimes. The outcome would decide whether he would spend the rest of his life in prison (Wisconsin has no death penalty) or whether he would be sent to a mental institution.

It was Valentine's Day afternoon, just two weeks after the trial began, when the jury deliberated for five hours and declared Dahmer sane on all fifteen counts. There had actually been sixteen murders in Wisconsin, but one body—the body of Steven Tuomi—was never recovered.

Sentencing was set for Monday, February 17. At sentencing, Dahmer read a statement in court asking that he receive no mercy. Judge Gram abided his request and sentenced him to fifteen consecutive life terms, equivalent to 957 years in prison, with no possibility of parole.

The Milwaukee County sheriff deputies handcuffed Dahmer and sent him back to Columbia.

Dahmer was returning to live among us for the rest of his life.

Eight
Back to Serve His Time

Stop being afraid of what you are about to suffer–for the devil will soon throw some of you into prison to test you. (The Revelation 2:10, TLB*)*

The media witnessed Dahmer's return to Columbia. The prison was open to them to reveal to the world where the notorious mass murderer would live out his remaining days. They saw the four guard towers, security systems, housing units with the inmates' cells, vocational areas, and the health-services facilities.

Before entering the unit, Dahmer again surrendered his street clothing and received the prerequisite institutional clothing–the same orange uniform he had before he went to trial.

Again, Dahmer was under heavy security. He returned to the glass tank, monitored twenty-four hours a day, with two cameras in his cell. Correctional officers continued to keep journals of all his activities and conversations.

Normally from 7 a.m. until 7:20 a.m., inmates may shave, but because Dahmer was on suicide watch, he was not given this privilege. After shave time, most prisoners in Desegregation Unit 1 were allowed recreation for about ninety minutes; again, Dahmer was not permitted to attend recreation. Walking around the glass tank and reading his mail were his only forms of recreation.

Warden Jeffrey P. Endicott and other Columbia officials wholly believed their facility was suitable for Dahmer and proclaimed this to the media the previous night. One question, however, had to have been on their minds: Could they guarantee Dahmer's safety from inmates who wanted to kill him or simply teach him a lesson?

Back to Serve His Time

There were still rumors, but now the rumors said Dahmer would be killed at Columbia because some of his victims had friends or relatives with inmates at the institution. The warden, security director, and deputy warden investigated these threatening rumors immediately. Security knew they couldn't keep Dahmer on suicide watch forever and, since the general population hated him so much, Dahmer's protection was a very consuming topic of conversation.

Every day during mail call, Jeff received bags of mail–hundreds of letters and each day the guards gave him twenty-five, the maximum allowed. The next day, in order to get twenty-five more letters, he had to return the ones from the prior day.

Life for the inmates in Units 4 through 9 seemed normal. But the lives of those housed on Units 1 and 2, the units nearest to Dahmer's cell, changed drastically because of our unfortunate proximity–and we weren't happy. Recreation in the gym was off-limits as was the hobby room and the music room. Even our library privileges were suspended.

We complained to the guards, but they wouldn't budge.

That evening we went to the canteen from 7:15 p.m. until 8:30 p.m. We had more uniformed officers than usual as escorts.

On February 19, inmates on Units 4 through 9 went to breakfast in the units' dayroom cafeterias while the cell doors for Units 1 and 2 remained closed. The sergeants proclaimed us "on lockdown until further notice." Our resentment grew. Dahmer's mere presence was taking away the miniscule scraps of freedom that we had.

That morning we received a lovely bag breakfast consisting of two boiled eggs, two slices of toast, two boxes of cereal, and two containers of milk. That night inmates on Units 4 through 9 attended Wednesday evening Catholic services, but not us. Lockdown.

Later that evening, a memo from the warden slid under our cell doors. "Officers have been noticing gang activities at various places such as the gym, school, and church," it read. "Therefore, there will be a search of each inmate's cell. Also each inmate in Units 1 and 2 will be questioned by captains and lieutenants."

Warden Endicott and the security director had *each* signed the memo.

The memo surprised us. First, *we* hadn't heard any talk of gang activity. Second, if the guards had noticed such activity, why didn't they stop it immediately like usual? The whole thing just increased our suspicions that Dahmer was the real reason for the lockdown and security just wouldn't admit it.

Lunch that day was served in bags, this time with two bologna sandwiches; raw carrot, celery, and radish sticks; two cookies; a carton of milk; and a cup of coffee.

It didn't take long before inmates in Units 4 through 9, the units *not* on lockdown, started asking about our units. Word reached relatives and friends outside the prison, who began calling the prison, inquiring about the lockdown status. The media-relations officer at Columbia stressed that Dahmer had nothing to do with the situation. Media reports incorrectly announced that the entire institution was on lockdown, not just Units 1 and 2.

Supper was served late that afternoon on Styrofoam trays: turkey, cold mashed potatoes, two slices of bread, one carton of milk, coffee, and one piece of fruit. After supper, inmates heard rumors that new gang members from the Black Gangster Disciples and Vice Lords just arrived at Columbia and claimed they wanted to take over the prison. Since Units 1 and 2 were gang units, we were sure that if there *were* gang members, they shared housing with us. Maybe there was something to the memo after all.

Finally, that night we could have visits from friends and family, but no other privileges.

On the morning of February 20, while Dahmer remained in his cell on Desegregation Unit 1, each prisoner in Units 1 and 2 left his cell, one at a time, handcuffed, and escorted to a multipurpose room on the unit. Officers interrogated us, asking questions mostly related to gang activities, but also wanting to know if we'd heard anything about any threats on Dahmer's life.

Every inmate was questioned for ten to twenty minutes before returning to his cell. The questioning went on all day.

That night, while the other inmates had recreation, we remained locked in our cells. By this point, we were pretty agitated. Most of the inmates on Units 1 and 2 have prison sentences ranging from five to seventy-five years and have a standard daily routine. Inmates don't like it when routine is upset.

Nine
Who is this Man, Dahmer?

Let me say this, then, speaking for the Lord: Live no longer as the unsaved do, for they are blinded and confused. Their closed hearts are full of darkness; they are far away from the life of God because they have shut their minds against him, and they cannot understand his ways. They don't care anymore about right and wrong and have given themselves over to impure ways. They stop at nothing, being driven by their evil minds and restless lusts. (Ephesians 4:17-19, TLB*)*

As I sat in my cell and read my Bible during those days after Dahmer joined our ranks, I found myself wondering over and over whether or not this man's soul could be saved. Oh, I knew if he would just ask for forgiveness and give his life over to Jesus the potential was there, but I wondered if Satan had such a powerful grip on him that all was lost.

Would Dahmer ever get to a point where he would ask forgiveness for his horrible sins? Would he even realize the immensity of them?

I wondered and I prayed.

During those first few weeks after Dahmer joined us, I had a *lot* of time on my hands, especially since we were on lockdown most of the time. Whenever I got the chance to go to the library, I read everything I could get my eyes on that discussed Dahmer's childhood or his life as a young man in Ohio and, later, Wisconsin. I read about Satanism and different cults, trying to find a correlation to Dahmer's despicable acts. I wanted to know how a person could do what he did to the bodies of the men and boys he murdered.

I read newspapers and magazines, did research, and took notes on a tablet in my cell. For me, the media couldn't write enough about Dahmer. To satisfy my need for information, I had to dig deeper into his background.

Who is this Man, Dahmer?

Jeffrey Lionel Dahmer was born on May 21, 1960, at Deaconess Hospital in Milwaukee to Joyce (Flint) and Lionel Dahmer. Jeff's mother and father had married the previous July in Milwaukee. Joyce, born in Chippewa Falls, Wisconsin, had a master's degree in counseling from the University of Wisconsin-Stout in Menomonie. Lionel received a degree in electrical engineering from Marquette University in Milwaukee.

Joyce Dahmer had a difficult pregnancy while carrying Jeff. Lionel said she suffered from psychiatric and environmental ailments throughout their son's childhood.

In 1966, the family moved to Ames, Iowa, where Lionel received a doctorate. He later got a job in Akron, Ohio, as a research chemist at PPG Industries and the family moved to Doylestown, Ohio. Joyce chose to stay home to raise Jeffrey. Family life was, by any standards, pretty normal during those days.

When Jeffrey was six, he started school at Hazel Harvey Elementary School in Barberton, Ohio. That same year, Jeffrey's younger brother, David, was born.

As a child, Jeffrey was polite and neat. Most people who knew them believed he had a good upbringing. The Dahmers weren't church-going people. The family religion was Protestant, but attending church wasn't important to the Dahmers.

Like many children his age, Jeff played baseball, had a job as a paperboy, and played games with children at school and in the neighborhood.

In 1968, the family moved to Bath, Ohio. It wasn't long before family life started to go downhill. During the next few years, Lionel and Joyce's marriage disintegrated. Jeffrey began to have difficulties with some of the children at school. They thought he was strange and, as children sometime do, bullied and teased him. Jeffrey began to spend more and more time alone in the woods, fascinated with nature.

When he was fourteen years old and in junior high, Jeff became even more of a loner. He alienated himself, and classmates stayed away completely because of his odd behavior. He did succeed academically, however. He was a smart student who received honors in science, his favorite subject. Not ironically, some of his science projects involved experimenting with animals.

In junior high and high school, Jeff became known as the class clown, but he also started drinking.

At Revere High School, he played the clarinet in the band. Later he joined the intramural tennis team, playing tennis from his sophomore year through his senior year, and worked on the school newspaper, *The Lantern*.

From 1975 through 1980, the years while Jeff was in high school, local authorities called on the Dahmer residence several times because of domestic disputes between Joyce and Lionel.

At fifteen, Jeff admitted fantasizing about homosexual activities, but never felt comfortable discussing this with his parents or peers. As a result, he retreated further and further into himself. Some wonder if school counselors or his parents knew about these thoughts and perhaps took action, would Jeff have turned into such a monster? Would his parents or professionals have been able to help him?

Regardless of speculation, that's not how history unfolded. Jeff kept everything hidden. He lied to himself and to those around him. He drank, probably in an effort to forget. Before long, Jeff's whole world became one of deceit and mind games.

At some point, Jeff became interested in Satanism. During his high school years, he invited the few friends he still had to his home for a séance. Fascinated by evil and the devil, Jeff tried his hardest to call Satan into their midst.

No one knows for sure just how much Jeff actually knew about Satanism, but some of the rituals he performed during his youth and, eventually, on his victims strangely resembled the practice. Later, interviews by authorities and psychiatrists after his arrest led them to believe Dahmer did these things more for personal pleasure and feelings of complete power over individuals rather than as an act of Satanism itself.

Lionel Dahmer filed for divorce from Joyce on November 4, 1977, near the beginning of Jeffrey's senior year, and moved into a motel. That didn't help family life; the confrontations between Jeff's parents continued. The divorce was final in 1978, just before Jeff graduated from high school.

That spring, Jeff asked a girl to prom. She accepted, although Jeff admitted later that he felt quite uncomfortable about his male role in the situation.

During the last few years of high school, Jeff's grades plunged and he graduated without honors.

Just a few weeks after graduation, on June 18, 1978, in Bath Township, Ohio, he killed his first victim, Steven Hicks.

Many accounts of Hicks' murder give an appearance that the murder was an accident, that Jeff didn't *intentionally* kill Hicks. Dahmer, likely lonely, just wanted to knock Hicks unconscious so he wouldn't leave.

Some wonder if that one accidental death was the pivotal turning point in Jeffrey Dahmer's legacy of horror.

That fall, Dahmer moved to Columbus, Ohio, to attend Ohio State University and major in business. His drinking continued quite heavily and because of his drinking, he was never able to keep his grades up. By semester's end, he was failing and dropped out.

In the meantime, Jeff's father began dating a woman named Shari and, on December 24, 1978, they were married. Two weeks later, Lionel, upset with Jeff for flunking out of college, dragged his son to the Army recruiter's office, and insisted that he enlist. Jeff did his basic training at Fort McClellan in Anniston, Alabama, and became a military police officer.

Jeff's years in the military were uneventful. He was transferred to Fort Sam Houston in San Antonio, Texas, where he completed a six-month course as a medical specialist. In July 1979, he went overseas to Baumholder in West Germany. Most people, authorities included, believe Jeff did not engage in any criminal or homosexual activities while in the Army.

In March 1981, at the age of twenty-one, Jeff was still drinking heavily and the Army discharged him under Chapter 9 of the code of military justice, the section that covers abuse of alcohol and drugs.

He went to Miami, where four months later, in the summer of 1981, he got a job at a sub sandwich shop. His income was so low that he couldn't afford decent housing and often slept on the beach. After six unsuccessful months in

Florida, his stepmother, Shari, called him, asking him return home. He stayed with Shari and Lionel until the following year.

The relationship between Lionel and Jeff was difficult. In 1982, Jeff left Ohio and, at his father's suggestion, moved to the Milwaukee suburb of West Allis to live with his paternal grandmother.

Jeff worked as a phlebotomist, a skill he learned in the Army, drawing blood samples at Milwaukee Blood Plasma.

In August 1982, not long after he arrived in Wisconsin, Jeff was arrested for exposing himself in a public area. Because of his arrest, he lost his job. He continued to live with his grandmother, but didn't land another job for more than two years. Finally, Jeff found a position at Ambrosia Chocolate Factory in downtown Milwaukee. His job responsibility surrounded mixing ingredients for chocolate products.

After twenty months of employment at Ambrosia Chocolate, he was arrested and convicted for masturbating on the riverbank of the Kinnickinnic River in Milwaukee. As a twenty-six year old, he received one year of probation by the Milwaukee Circuit Court and underwent psychological therapy.

During his therapy, a psychiatrist diagnosed him with a schizoid personality wherein a person loses contact with reality, experiences a disintegrated personality, and may even have hallucinations.

The following year, 1987, Dahmer started frequenting gay taverns in Milwaukee, including Club 219, where he often hung out after work and on weekends. In September, he met his second victim, Steven Tuomi. Tuomi was the victim whose body was stuffed into a suitcase, chopped up, and dispersed. Tuomi's body was never found.

Around the same time, Jeff started reading books on Cryonics. Cryonics is the practice of freezing a dead, diseased human in hopes of resurrection at some point in the future, after finding a cure for whatever disease may have afflicted them. The concept fascinated Jeff.

Jeff's murderous compulsion was in a fledgling stage. In April of 1988, after Jeff had already killed two more victims, he met Ronald Flowers in Zion, Illinois. He brought the young Flowers to his grandmother's house, but Jeff's grandmother saw them in the living room and asked Jeff not to bring his friends home anymore. In fact, she told Jeff she thought it was time he got his own apartment. Flowers didn't know it at the time, but Jeff's grandmother likely saved his life.

When Jeff was arrested in 1988 for sexually assaulting a minor, after his single day of freedom associated with living on his own, Jeff's father hired Attorney Gerald Boyle to represent his son for the first time. Jeff, convicted, received five years' probation and one year at the House of Corrections as part of the work-release program.

His brush with the law didn't deter Jeff. He continued his spree and actually accelerated the rate at which he was killing. In June and through July of 1990, he averaged killing one victim per week.

It was shocking to learn that those horrendous murders were committed while Dahmer was under the supervision of a probation officer. Dahmer's ability to fool not only his victims, but authority figures as well, with believable stories was perhaps the reason he was able to carry on his monstrous madness for so long. That each of his victims *willingly* entered his apartment reflect his uncanny ability to lie and manipulate. As Dahmer pointed out to authorities later, none of his victims seemed to suffer any pain as they were heavily drugged into unconsciousness before their deaths.

Near the end of July 1990, Tracy Edwards famously managed escape from Jeff's grasp, ultimately leading to his arrest. Dahmer's world of evil was finally penetrated; his house of horror, lust, deceit, murder, and sexual deprivation crumbled around him.

During his trial, Dahmer wondered aloud if there was such a thing as a satanic influence and if it was possible that evil spirits controlled him during his reign of revulsion. Dahmer obviously knew about Satan but I questioned if he knew about God. Maybe, if he had only let the power of God influence him and help him fight evil, things would have been different.

Ten
The Great Weapons Search

They will be rounded up like prisoners and imprisoned in a dungeon until they are tried and condemned. (Isaiah 24:22, TLB)

The prison rules and procedures are set forth in the Department of Corrections' *Rules and Procedures* handbook, a hefty book given to each prisoner upon his arrival at Columbia. There are basically eight major offenses an inmate can commit:

1. An offense against bodily security: battery, threats, fighting, or sexual assault;
2. An offense against institution security: inciting a riot, organizing group resistance, including petitions, or disguising your identity;
3. An offense against orders: disobeying orders, being disrespectful, lying about the staff, or getting involved with an enterprise or fraudulent activity;
4. An offense against property: damage or alteration of property, unauthorized transfer of property;
5. Contraband offenses: possession of drug paraphernalia; possession, manufacture, and alteration of weapons; unauthorized use of the mail;
6. Movement offenses: leaving assigned area, being in an unassigned area, entry of another inmate's quarters;
7. Offenses against safety and health: misuse of prescription medication, disfigurement; or
8. Miscellaneous offenses: use of intoxicants, gambling, refusal to work or attend school, violation of institution policies and procedures.

For serious violations, such as disobeying an order, possession or use of drugs or weapons, fighting or stealing, the inmate is sent to temporary lockup.

The Great Weapons Search

When allegations like this surface, an inmate receives a due-process hearing where he is provided an opportunity to call witnesses, including fellow inmates, staff members, or officers. He also can choose a staff advocate and cross-examine that staff member at his hearing. The hearing by the adjustment committee normally takes place within two to twenty-one days after receiving the conduct report.

After the adjustment committee meets, an inmate can appeal the decision to the inmate complaint investigator (ICI). The ICI will make an impartial investigation of the inmate's complaint and the inmate will receive a copy of the ICI's decision. If the ICI's decision is not to an inmate's satisfaction, he may file an appeal with the Department of Justice's Correction Complaint Examiner (CCE) in Madison.

I tell you all this because I experienced, first-hand, the internal legal prison system, charged with No. 5: contraband, possession of weapons.

It was Friday, February 21, 1992. We were served breakfast in bags that morning and, right after we ate, inmates on Units 1 and 2 were handcuffed and escorted to the dayroom. While in the dayroom, officers searched our cells for weapons. Word spread quickly that Dahmer was going to be moving to a regular solitary-confinement cell and officials wanted to search cells to ensure nobody had weapons to harm him.

Security guards and officers meticulously combed each cell from top to bottom: window, walls, bed, toilet, sink, desk, and stool. They went through our personal letters, court papers, magazines, and books. They searched clothing, shoes, and personal items. Officers wrote reports on anyone who had any violation against any institutional policy or procedure.

At about 3:30 p.m., officers came to Cell 35—my cell. Handcuffed, they escorted me to the dayroom. During their search, an officer found a razor blade wedged between the window and the wall. The blade wasn't mine; I was certain a prisoner who occupied my cell sometime before me left it behind. Nevertheless, I was not in a position to discuss my innocence, nor was I even asked.

I was immediately sent to Desegregation Unit 2. I relinquished my regular clothing and received orange clothes, sheets, a blanket, pillow, and pillowcase.

The door slammed on Cell 2. I was in temporarily lockup until further notice.

Around 9:30 p.m., Officer Hoffman, the officer who found the razor blade in my cell, gave me a copy of Adult Conduct Report No. 392098, typed on Department of Health and Social Services, Division of Corrections letterhead. The report listed the charges brought against me. They were:

- Damage or alteration to property;
- Possession, manufacture, and alteration of weapons; and
- Possession of contraband, miscellaneous.

The officer wrote, "On the above date, 2/21/92, at 3:35 p.m., while searching inmate's Martin, Calvin #139891, HU-2 [Housing Unit 2], Cell 35, I found a razor blade that has been removed from a razor. It also has tape placed across one side of the razor blade. The razor blade was concealed in the upper right side of the window screen."

After hearing the allegations, I was really upset. I was *finally* turning my life around, making things better, and here I was, already incarcerated on modified charges and now blamed for a crime I did *not* commit.

I tried calmly explaining to Officer Hoffman that I was innocent and the evidence against me was from a prior inmate. I remember telling him specifically that it wasn't my razor blade and that I hadn't even been in that cell long. I relayed that I had heard the inmate housed there prior to me shaved with that specific type of razor and must have left the blade there. The razor in question was a "tractor blade" and I didn't shave with that type of blade.

I thought it made sense and was easy to see the rationale I presented. How *could* it be my razor blade? I also pointed out that I wasn't exactly a neat freak. We all knew it was the guys with sloppy, messy cells who got surprise searches all the time. I connected the dots for him, citing that if I *was* intentionally hiding a weapon, I would have kept my cell spotless to avoid frequent searches.

I rambled on and on, trying in vain to get the officer to believe me. My effort didn't seem to matter much. There wasn't anything he could do, whether he believed me or not.

I requested that Officer Hoffman check with the canteen for orders turned in by the inmate who had previously been in Cell 35. If he ordered those tractor-type blades from the canteen, I was positive I could convince the committee of my innocence.

The officer merely relayed that I would be granted due process.

The next day, February 23, I sent a note to the warden, explained the battery of things I had already tried to tell Officer Hoffman. I also wrote a letter to the security director, Mr. Davidson.

On February 24, I received a memo from Warden Endicott that stated: "I have received your note of 2/23/92 regarding a conduct report you received. It is clear from your letter that you have not been seen by the Due Process Committee. It would be inappropriate for me to become involved in this matter at this time. If and when you are found guilty of this offense, you do have the right to appeal the Due Process Committee's decision to the warden's office. I will become involved in the matter at that time."

I also received a memo from Captain Marv Prieve, the security director. The subject was "Pending Conduct Report." Captain Prieve's memo stated: "I have received your letter to Mr. Davidson, dated 2/23/92. That conduct report was reviewed and determined to be a major offense. You will be afforded an opportunity to call witnesses and/or present evidence at your due-process hearing, which is scheduled for March 11, 1992, in Desegregation Unit 1. Until that time you will stay in DS-2, cell number two. If you are dissatisfied with the outcome of the hearing, you do have appeal rights."

I remained in solitary confinement, Cell 2, from February 21 through March 11.

Being in solitary confinement, or temporary lockup, was almost as drastic as going to prison in the first place. It was a difficult adjustment. We couldn't even socialize during meals, which we received through the trap on the door. Because all inmates on Units 1 and 2 were still on lockdown, all meals were in bags or on Styrofoam trays.

There was no television or a radio.

Recreation was three times a week instead of daily. I could have three showers a week and one ten-minute phone call.

Knowing I was innocent, I was frustrated. Maybe beyond frustrated. I wanted to attend school, group meetings, canteen, recreation, and chapel services. I wanted to do the things that not only kept me occupied, but things that kept me on the right path. I wanted things that helped me in my journey to become a *good* person. Instead, I was confined to a cell.

Days were long; nights were longer. I spent my new-found "down-time" consumed with praying and reading my Bible, which was getting dog-eared with use. The long, cold days of February slowly turned into March.

Then, just as suddenly, my life became interesting. A new prisoner moved into DS-2, Cell 1, right next-door to mine.

Eleven
And So It Begins

If you will stir up this inner power, you will never be afraid to tell others about our Lord, or to let them know that I am your friend even though I am here in jail for Christ's sake. You will be ready to suffer with me for the Lord, for he will give you strength in suffering. (II Timothy 1:8, TLB)

On the afternoon of Monday, March 2, 1992, Dahmer transferred from the glass tank in Desegregation Unit 1 to Cell 1 in Desegregation Unit 2, right next to mine.

When Jeffrey arrived, I was reading my Bible and trying to talk with inmates in other cells about scriptures. At that point, I'd only been a Christian for a year and a half so I was by no means a biblical scholar. I enjoyed discussions about the Bible. Some inmates were believers; others were not.

Before Jeff arrived, some of the inmates on our tier, like inmates and citizens everywhere, were saying bad things about him. The majority were completely convinced he was a racist and hated minorities.

The scene was set and it wasn't exactly a "welcoming committee." Immediately after Dahmer arrived, verbal abuse and threats against him began.

"If I ever see you alone, I'll kill you, you racist pig!" one inmate shouted.

The shouts and jeers escalated. Dahmer never said a word. One inmate asked what he did with all his victims. No response. More questions and jeers flew at him like, "Did the male parts taste good?" or "did you have a feast with all those feet you had on hand?"

Dahmer remained silent.

The questions, swearing, threats, jokes, and comments continued and got louder. I tried to defuse the situation and asked the other inmates to keep the noise down so I could talk to a few people. Some guy shouted at me, "You're not the only one who wants to talk. Other people do, too."

The noise continued all afternoon.

At 4 p.m., we had standing count. Supper, served on a plastic tray, passed through the door traps at 4:30 p.m. When Jeff received his tray, some of the inmates started yelling again. "Does this taste better than human meat? Which one tastes better?"

As before, Dahmer didn't respond.

They continued.

"Hey, Jeff, do you prefer dark meat or white meat?"

"He definitely preferred dark meat over white meat!" one of the white guys jeered.

"Brother, Jeff consumed more red than white meat," said one Hispanic inmate, laughing.

No sound came from Cell 1.

After a few minutes, one guy shouted, "Hey, Jeff, how's the corpse?"

That time, much to everyone's surprise, Dahmer replied. "Chunky," he said, "delicious and tasty."

After supper, an officer collected all the trays and gave Dahmer his medication. I learned later that he'd been taking the same prescription drugs for a couple years, prescribed by a psychiatrist after his sexual-assault charge. The two drugs were Lorazepam and Doxepin. Lorazepam is a drug used to control anxiety and acts as a relaxant. It's for people with high stress or nervous conditions. Doxepin is an anti-depressant or sleep aid.

He received both drugs four times a day.

Right after supper, the clamor started again. "Did you eat all the meat on your tray, you animal?" They continued calling him a racist and making other derogatory remarks that crossed their minds.

I don't know why, but I had enough. "Hey, that man has already been given his time," I told the outspoken inmates. "He's being punished for what he did. He got caught for all his wrong-doing and now he's doing time for the rest of his life. So let the man rest. He's entitled to that. He's entitled to be left alone."

And So It Begins

Even Dahmer didn't deserve the onslaught of abuse. As a Christian, I believed that even though this man did horrible things he was still just a sinner, just like the rest of us. In God's eyes, we are all His children, and wishing pain and hurt upon someone else makes us no better. For that matter, who were we to judge him?

I actually felt sorry for Dahmer. Of course, I didn't agree with what he did, but he was obviously troubled. Dahmer walked into the lion's den but I decided I wasn't going to let him go alone.

Someone hollered to me from down the line. "Brother, I don't know why you're taking up for that racist! He killed all those Brothers. Dahmer don't give a fuck about you, just like he didn't care about those he tricked into going to his apartment and then killed. And then what he did to them afterwards! Man, I don't get how you can stick up for him!"

They all started in again, using profanity to try to get Dahmer to talk, but a   ord. Finally, an officer barked to quiet down.

ments bothered me; I wondered if they bothered Jeff

ious about him. Not just his history, but I wondered

king. Was he feeling bad, scared, or hateful? Was he

back and start over? Did he know about God or Satan?

t people up?

Questions kept popping into my head.

It was strange to think that Jeffrey Dahmer, one of the most notorious serial killers of all time, was right on the other side of my cell wall . . . just inches away. I was within speaking distance to a man that most considered a monster.

Then it hit me. I started to believe that Dahmer was next to me for a reason. Perhaps this was the work of the Lord. The questions I left in his hands seemed to be answered. I began to think I was *supposed* to talk to him, get to know him, and help him get to know God.

Later that evening, an officer asked if we wanted to take showers and clean our cells. He started at Cell 1. Even though the shower was across from

Dahmer's cell, which meant Jeff wouldn't have to walk in front of anyone else, Dahmer didn't want to take a shower, nor did he want to clean his cell.

I was next in line for the shower. Only one inmate could shower at a time. When I came out and walked past his cell, I looked in the glass window and saw him sitting on his stool, reading letters.

As I passed, I hit his door, which was my way of saying "hello." He responded with a nonchalant, "Hey." I was glad he was willing to be friendly at least.

Then the full scope of events hit me. This whole mess of being in solitary confinement for a crime I did not commit, winding up in the only cell next to Jeffrey Dahmer . . . every step that I took to get to this very point and the steps that I was pushed to by no fault of my own were God's plan. God knew I was a new Christian and Jeff was a lost soul. God brought us together to learn about Christianity *together*. I had a perfect opportunity to talk to Dahmer and I could help open his eyes to the blessed light and limitless forgiveness. I didn't know how I was going to start or even what I was going to say, but somehow I knew I had to help him.

After my shower, other inmates passed Dahmer's cell. They'd stand in front of his door and stare at him, as if he was a caged animal on display. The stainless-steel shower walls across from Dahmer's cell were as shiny as a mirror. I could look out the window of my door and see everyone coming and going.

Around 8 p.m., the officer on duty brought requested items from the unit supply, along with more mail.

At 9 p.m., we had standing count. I read more about Dahmer in a few newspapers and magazines, stories that told in gruesome detail what he'd done to those whose lives he stole. I was so curious to know *why* . . . why he did it and why he did it the *way* he did it. I finally decided to try to talk to Jeff. I knew I would have to do so quietly, it was already after 9 p.m. and we weren't supposed to talk.

Inmates who were allowed could watch TV or listen to their radios as late as they want, but all electronics required headphones so the unit was completely quiet after 9 p.m. This, also, is an institutional rule. It would be noisy at night if every inmate had their volume on and tuned in to a different TV channel or radio station.

It was my first night with Dahmer in the cell next to mine. He was in Cell 1, so there was no one on the other side of him–just the stairs that led to our tier. If *anyone* would be able to talk to him privately, it could only be the person in Cell 2. . . me.

A twelve-foot-long concrete block wall separated us, but there were vents in that wall near the ceiling. In the steel doors of our cells, there was a speaker with holes in it so sound could pass from the cell to the hallway. If anyone tried to talk through that, everyone would hear.

I sat on my bed and stared at the gray wall separating us, I looked up at the vents at the top of my cell. I knew those vents led directly into Dahmer's cell. My eyes trailed down toward my metal sink attached to the wall. My curiosity overtook my fear. I was certain, if I stood on the sink, I could get close enough to the vents to talk to him quietly.

I wondered if he would talk back.

I took a deep breath and could feel my palms getting sweaty. I stood up, went over the sink, put both hands onto the sides, and hoisted myself up onto it. The pipes beneath the shiny metal creaked slightly under the new, unwanted addition of my weight. I steadied myself and leaned toward the wall. I listened for just a moment to see if I could hear anything.

Nothing but silence.

I had to remind myself that Dahmer was *just a man*, a sinner like all the rest of us–lost and looking for light. He was not something inhuman. I could do this. I could try to engage Jeffery Dahmer in a conversation.

I whispered into the vents near the ceiling that went into Dahmer's cell.

"Hey, Jeff, mind if I ask you some questions?" I focused on keeping my voice even and friendly.

"I don't care," he replied flatly.

I was surprised he answered. He had been so resolutely quiet before, enduring gibes and questions and only uttering one response. I decided to start with some general questions. "So, how are you doing over there?" I cringed at the awkwardness of the question, but we had to start somewhere.

"Been better," he responded. I could tell he was upset but I was glad he was willing to talk.

I couldn't talk to him about God right away; I figured I needed to build up some kind of rapport. Then, when he was comfortable and I knew what to expect from him, I could tell him about the goodness of God.

I had to ask the one specific thing that had haunted my mind since his arrest. "Jeff, why did you target minorities instead of your own race?"

Dahmer didn't answer for a few moments. He must have smirked before he spoke because I could hear the sarcasm in his voice, "Why? Because they're all ignorant, they should all die. I was cleaning the earth of those maggots and I believe I did my share. Also, if everyone killed as many as I did, there would be no more niggers, spicks, or gooks in America."

His voice got louder, intentional, so everyone could hear him. "So do it, people, before it's too late!"

I felt blood rush to my head and I felt my hands curl into a fist. Racism was one of the things that I loathed. I admit, at that moment I wanted to beat that murdering racist. I wondered if he knew that I was a black man but then I figured it probably wouldn't have made his answer any different. Admittedly, his angry outburst surprised me; he had been so quiet before.

A few other inmates heard part of our discussion, especially Dahmer's loud, racist statement, and started in again with profanities, threats, and shouting.

I took a deep breath, let my rage settle, calmed myself, and remembered that I am a Christian. I put my head down, rested my forehead against the cold cement wall, and closed my eyes. I started to pray for the man in Cell 1. I prayed that sometime soon he would accept God into his life and let go of the hate that still consumed him. I prayed I would be able to help him.

The noise from the other inmates escalated and two officers came up the stairs, yelling for us to pipe down. I quickly jumped off the sink. Everyone lowered their voices until the officers left before taunting Dahmer again.

Once again, he didn't respond.

I listened. When quiet returned, I climbed back up on the sink. I had more that I wanted to know, and this time I had more courage.

"Why did you confess to the authorities everything about the killings?" I asked. "Why did you give them all the details of the rituals and the methods you used to carry out the murders?"

I heard him take a deep breath. "Because I find it extremely sexual to go over the crimes I committed, and I get off telling exactly how I took the worthless lives of those people," he said. "Why shouldn't I be proud and tell others? I only did what needed to be done and I told them of all seventeen because I'm proud of my attempt to rid the planet of that type of trash."

I could hear anger in his voice. I whispered back, "Well, you were caught red-handed after Tracy Edwards broke away and told the police. You must have known you were going to get caught." I regretted talking so loudly because other inmates started up again with more threats.

A pattern had developed. It was a pattern dictated by Dahmer. He'd decided, for some reason, to only talk to me that night if no one else was talking. He wasn't about to respond to the loud, angry racket from the other inmates.

A few minutes later, when the quiet again returned, I asked another question weighing on my mind: "Why did you keep the skulls with the skin removed? And why did you *paint* them?"

"Each skull represented a life I took," he said. "They're proof, along with the photographs, that I did my part.

"Personally, I found the skulls somewhat erotic. I could sit and stare or fondle them for hours, fantasizing about killing more people. I really liked the skulls. Plus, I knew that if the police ever found a *real* skull in my possession, it would be confiscated. The paint was a form of disguise so they wouldn't be taken."

I wondered if Jeff realized how crazy he seemed or if he even remotely understood what he had done was wrong. Jeff always talked loud enough so a few of the inmates could hear what he was saying and, every time he talked, they'd start yelling and swearing and threatening his life.

I had spent a lot of time keeping up with the Dahmer case. There were so many questions flirting through my head, waiting to be asked. "Why did you keep the lungs, intestines, kidney, arm muscles, and hearts in your refrigerator and freezer?"

"It was food," he said, "and it would have been eaten if I'd have had the time to do it. Also, I could take the parts out whenever I needed the rush I got from chopping them up. They were an asset, man."

Hearing him speak, letting the impact of his words wash over me; it was hard to keep him "human" versus "monster" in my head. My insides lurched with every word he uttered. I told myself to keep it together, reminding myself over and over that this man needs Jesus in his life. There was so much hatred in him. I prayed for him again. I also prayed for me. I asked God to help me touch Jeff's heart with His goodness and peace. Talking to him that evening showed me *exactly* how twisted and tortured Jeffrey Dahmer really was.

I sat down on my bed and thought back to September 1990 when I accepted Jesus as my Lord and Savior. I recalled Levy, the prisoner who had brought me to the Lord, and wondered if I had the strength and ability to guide another soul to Jesus as Levy had guided me. I remembered all the church services and Bible classes I'd attended. At that moment, I decided to talk to Jeff about God and his Son, about the faith that had changed my life and my heart.

I knew the best way to reach this man was to start with something he'd understand—Satan. I decided to share some Bible scriptures with him that showed the power the devil could have over us.

I opened my Bible to Isaiah and reread to myself the verses I'd read so many times before. I read the verses aloud to Jeff.

Your might and power are gone; they are buried with you. All the pleasant music in your palace has ceased; now maggots are your sheet, worms your blanket! How you are fallen from heaven, O Lucifer, son of the morning! How you are cut down to the ground—mighty though you were against the nations of the world. For you said to yourself, 'I will ascend to heaven and rule the angels. I will take the highest throne. I will preside on the Mount of Assembly far away in the north. I will climb to the highest heavens and be like the Most High.' But instead, you will be brought down to the pit of hell, down to its lowest depths. Everyone there will stare at you and ask, 'Can this be the one who shook the earth and the kingdoms of the world?' (Isaiah 14:11-16, TLB)

After reading those verses aloud, I felt better, like some of the evil in the cell had lifted. It gave me courage. I asked Jeff if he had his own Bible. He said his personal Bible was with the rest of his things. The only Bible he had was one the prison supplied.

I told him to read Ezekiel, which says:

Then this further message came to me from the Lord: 'Son of dust, weep for the king of Tyre. Tell him, the Lord God says: You were the perfection of wisdom and beauty. You were in Eden, the garden of God; your clothing was bejeweled with every precious stone–ruby, topaz, diamond, chrysolite, onyx, jasper, sapphire, carbuncle, and emerald–all in beautiful settings of finest gold. They were given to you on the day you were created. I appointed you to be the anointed guardian cherub. You had access to the holy mountain of God. You walked among the stones of fire.

'You were perfect in all you did from the day you were created until that time when wrong was found in you. Your great wealth filled you with internal turmoil and you sinned. Therefore, I cast you out of the mountain of God like a common sinner. I destroyed you, O overshadowing cherub, from the midst of the stones of fire. Your heart was filled with pride because of all your beauty; you corrupted your wisdom for the sake of your splendor. Therefore I have cast you down to the ground and exposed you helpless before the curious gaze of kings. You defiled your holiness with lust for gain; therefore I brought forth fire from your own actions and let it burn you to ashes upon the earth in the sight of all those watching you. All who know you are appalled at your fate; you are an example of horror; you are destroyed forever.' (Ezekiel 28:11-19, *TLB*)

Jeff didn't respond after I read that passage. I hoped he was thinking about what he did and, now that he was in prison for life, probably felt like he was "destroyed forever."

I didn't let up. Not yet. This time I turned to the fire-and-brimstone chapter in the Bible—The Revelation 12:9-12. I wanted him to understand how Satan ended up on earth and about his power of evil over us. I explained to Jeff that Satan originally was known as Lucifer and was the highest of God's created beings and, in fact, God anointed him to lead the worship in heaven.

I told him how Lucifer became prideful and wanted to be like God, to take his place on the throne of heaven. Lucifer led an unsuccessful army. God's retribution was swift. Lucifer, now known as Satan, found himself exiled from heaven along with one-third of the angels who followed him. He was forced to wander the earth until Jesus returned and cast Satan into hell.

I believed that Dahmer worshipped Satan in some fashion during his vicious crimes. Either that, or Satan had taken control of his soul and pushed him to continue his horrible crimes against mankind.

"Satan does not own the earth," I told him. "It belongs to God. Scriptures tell us that Satan is a real, invisible power behind some of the world's rulers. Satan was the power behind Tyre, Babylon, Greece, and Rome. He is also the power behind many of our nations."

I told Jeff to read John 8:44, John 10:10, II Corinthians 11:14-15, and I Peter 5:8. I also mentioned The Revelation 12:10, which was part of the scriptures I had just read to him. I wanted him to reread it and understand the fall of Satan and how he turned from good to evil. I wanted Jeff to see how Satan had influenced him, but I also wanted to explain how God's goodness and love was much more powerful. I deeply wanted Jeff to understand he could save himself if he only looked to God.

After I told him which scriptures to read, I realized we'd talked for a long time. I decided to start keeping a journal of our talks. Through a journal, I could write down what Jeff said and look it over later, maybe find new verses to help him.

As I fell asleep that night, I prayed desperately for the tortured soul in Cell 1.

Here are the verses I asked Jeff to read that night:

For you are the children of your father the devil and you love to do the evil things he does. He was a murderer from the beginning and a hater of the truth–there is not an iota of truth in him. When he lies, it is perfectly normal; for he is the father of liars. (John 8:44, *TLB*)

The thief's purpose is to steal, kill and destroy. My purpose is to give life in all its fullness. (John 10:10, *TLB*)

Satan can change himself into an angel of light, so it is no wonder his servants can do it too, and seem like godly ministers. In the end they will get every bit of punishment their wicked deeds deserve. (II Corinthians 11:14-15, *TLB*)

Be careful–watch out for attacks from Satan, your great enemy. He prowls around like a hungry, roaring lion, looking for some victim to tear apart. (I Peter 5:8, *TLB*)

Then I heard a loud voice shouting across the heavens, "It has happened at last! God's salvation and the power and the rule, and the authority of his Christ are finally here; for the Accuser of our brothers has been thrown down from heaven onto earth–he accused them day and night before our God." (The Revelation 12:10, *TLB*)

Twelve
Dahmer's Private Hell

I live in terror now. They hold me in contempt and my prosperity has vanished as a cloud before a strong wind. My heart is broken. Depression haunts my days. My weary nights are filled with pain as though something were relentlessly gnawing at my bones. All night long I toss and turn, and my garments bind about me. God has thrown me into the mud. I have become as dust and ashes. (Job 30:15-19, TLB)

Tuesday, March 3, 1992.

Units 1 and 2 remained on lockdown. That meant yet another non-social breakfast in a bag. After breakfast, Jeff got his medication and an officer brought the cart with shaving equipment. When the officer collected the razors, he inspected the blades to make sure all were still intact. Jeff, being new, likely didn't even know the razors were inspected.

At 11 a.m., officers brought our mail. Stacks of mail, all for Dahmer, filled one entire table in the cafeteria.

At 11:30 a.m., lunch was served. Jeff ate everything on his tray.

After lunch, the psychologist came to talk to Dahmer. He told him that they'd be setting up a regular weekly visit.

Between noon and 2:30 p.m., inmates received items they had ordered from the prison store. When you're in Desegregation Unit 2, you can only order items from the canteen on Fridays, and since Dahmer came to the unit on Monday, he had to wait all week for that privilege.

We watched TV for the rest of the afternoon, with the exception of Dahmer, who wasn't allowed any electronics. In this unit, the only hope you had of leaving your cell during the day was if you had a scheduled appointment or a visitor.

There was the usual security shift change at 2:30 p.m., the 4 p.m.

inmates' standing count, followed by supper. While collecting the supper trays, an officer brought Dahmer his medication. Once again, I saw that Dahmer had eaten everything on his tray. The man had an appetite. I, on the other hand, did not. I couldn't bring myself to eat much. A lot was going through my mind and my appetite suffered.

At 8 p.m. an officer brought requested supplies to the tier. He also collected any letters the inmates needed mailed. At 9 p.m. there was another standing count.

That night when things were quiet, I decided to ask Dahmer more questions. There was just *so much* I wanted to know and I couldn't help but ask him. There were many things about him I actually understood, like compulsion, anger, and addiction. I understood fear, hate, and desire. I knew there were similarities between us, similarities between all the inmates here. Every inmate, in my opinion, gave in to our desires; we all had a general lack of self restraint. But there were so many other things he did that were beyond my level of comprehension. Things he did were downright disturbing and gruesome and criminal, even from a criminal's standpoint.

It wasn't that I just wanted to pick his brain and ask about his crimes or try to examine his psyche. I also wanted to ask him about other things, like his interests and hobbies and all of the other things that make us "human."

And, of course, I wanted to talk more about the scriptures and see if I could bring more of the word of God into his life. If Jeff saw and understood God, I believed it would change him. He could let go of his hate and his fear and open himself up to love and forgiveness.

That night, I asked Jeff about his interests. He told me he liked cars and traveling. He said he loved sports and his favorite sports teams were the Green Bay Packers for football, the Milwaukee Bucks for basketball, and the Milwaukee Admirals for hockey. He also said he enjoyed drinking Ole English 100 in forty-ounce bottles. He was open about the fact that he *really* liked smoking pot and drinking.

I wanted to avoid sounding like an interrogator, so I asked all my questions calmly and casually. I let my general curiosity flavor the questions because I knew he would "hear" it in my tone. Finally, I asked, "Why did you take photographs of your mutilated and dismembered victims?"

Jeffrey answered in an equally casual tone, as if we were talking about pictures of sunsets or family vacations. "Like I said before, I like to look at pornographic pictures to get myself aroused. Then I'd want to hurt someone and victims weren't readily available, but I always had pictures of my previous victims to get off with. I was mystified by the look a person got in their eyes when they knew they were going to die."

The statement confused me. Dahmer testified in court that he drugged all his victims and they were unconscious when he killed them. If they were drugged, would they be coherent enough to feel the fear associated with knowing death was looming? I had an urge to ask, but I didn't feel like going into that subject anymore with him.

I was suddenly glad there was a thick cement wall separating us. My relationship with Dahmer, if you can call it that at this point, was confusing. I was obsessed with curiosity surrounding who he was and how he could do the vile things he did. Conversely, picturing him hovering over his victims, aroused by his own acts, and watching them die, disgusted me.

Jeff continued, making sure to pepper his statements with some racist comment here or there to provoke the other inmates, "The pictures of the dead bodies were my tokens to prove that I did attempt to rid this earth of niggers, gooks, and spicks. I did my best."

No Jeff, I said to myself, *you took those pictures because you're insane.* At that time, I believed he truly was insane. He *had* to be insane. What kind of sane person would do those things?

Now, when I look back on our conversations and letters and everything I read about him, I don't believe he was insane at all. I'm sure there was a sickness of some sort in his brain, but he wasn't insane. Jeff knew exactly what he was doing and he knew it was wrong. He just didn't care. He also didn't understand the power of God's forgiveness and that he could have started his life over at any time, if he had just turned his life over to God.

The questions burned on my tongue now. "Why did you photograph the men and boys nude before you killed them or performed the various sex acts?" I asked.

Dahmer's voice was flat and matter of fact. "I used the photographs as a personal means of sexual enticement, just as any *straight* man would want pictures of females. I'd get completely aroused by them."

I assumed that Jeff had heard that type of question a lot since his arrest, so he was probably used to answering it. It bothered me that he didn't seem remorseful whatsoever about his crimes. It was as if he had no emotional connection to what he had done, he was completely removed from any sort of empathy for the lives he stole and the families he'd destroyed.

I decided to change the topic to something more helpful to Jeff and more important to my final hope for him, so I asked him, "Did you know Satan is a liar and a murderer? He wants to kill us, to deceive us, and he whispers false witness to us. Satan causes us to make bad decisions. Satan destroys our power to witness to God. He makes us ineffective Christians while putting us in bondage."

I felt excited as I said it, as though God was there helping me find the right words, giving me courage and strength. I thought about Levy and how he must have felt when he was teaching me about God and forgiveness.

Jeff was quiet, but I knew he was listening, so I continued. "Demons are fallen angels who joined forces with Satan. They're full of misfortune. They are nothing more than creatures that follow a merciless master with no purpose. They have no place to call home and therefore just wander the earth trying to get us into trouble. Demons are everywhere, Jeff, tempting us every day. We have to fight their temptations."

Then Jeff spoke up, but quietly this time, almost as if he wasn't even talking to me, but to himself. "Man, why are you preaching to me? Why do you care whether or not I know about this stuff? What difference does it make to you or to me?"

I could tell that Jeff was trying to say that he thought his soul was lost … a lost cause. He probably believed that men like him didn't deserve heaven and definitely wouldn't end up going to heaven. Jeff probably thought no one cared about him now.

"Jeff," I answered, "although I haven't been a Christian for long and I don't know everything there is to know about how to be a good Christian, I do know that it is important to help people, to find the good in others and help them see that goodness inside of them. What I've learned about God is that He is forgiving and loving, even when men go astray. As long as you believe and turn to God, He has the power to save any man. Learning about our Lord has changed my life and made me into a better person, and I think that if you learn and see, He can help you, too."

Jeff and I remained silent for awhile. I wanted Jeff to know that I cared about his soul, that I wasn't just there to question the horrible crimes he committed or try to find some grand epiphany to explain his actions. I wanted him to know that I could help him find the good person hidden inside of him. I prayed for a moment, asking God to give me strength.

Finally, I asked Jeff to open his Bible and read Luke 11:24-26 and Mark 5:10-13. I waited. I knew he hadn't moved, and for a moment, I thought he was ignoring me. Then I heard him search for his Bible. He opened it and began slowly flipping through the wispy pages. I smiled to myself. I wanted him to read about how the demons in this world can possess men and women, and how they can even inhabit other living things. I believed Satan possessed Jeff and just never let him go.

When a demon is cast out of a man, it goes to the deserts, searching there for rest; but finding none, it returns to the person it left, and finds that its former home is all swept and clean. Then it goes and gets seven other demons more evil than itself, and they all enter the man. And so the poor fellow is seven times worse off than he was before. (Luke 11:24-26, *TLB*)

Then the demons begged him again and again not to send them to some distant land. Now as it happened there was a huge herd of hogs rooting around on the hill above the lake. "Send us into those hogs," the demons begged. And Jesus gave them permission. Then the evil spirits came out of the man and entered the hogs, and the entire herd plunged down the steep hillside into the lake and drowned. (Mark 5:10-13, *TLB*)

Jeff and I continued to talk through the vents in our cells. We talked late into the evening. Finally, I still had some letters to write, I said good night.

I prayed for his soul again before drifting off to sleep and I hoped he was thinking about those demons that had entered his heart, mind, and soul.

I wondered if Jeff understood what I had told him or any of the scriptures I'd read or asked him to read. More so, I wondered if he even cared.

During the next few days, as our conversations continued, it was more evident to me that Dahmer's personality was weak. He was easily intimidated and fear seemed to fill his soul.

Although protected in his cell, I could tell the other inmates seemed daunting to him, especially the ones who were so radical in the way they ridiculed and swore at him. His fear seemed to frustrate him. Many times daily, especially when they were passing by his cell, inmates would threaten him or spit on his window. They never let up.

I could easily imagine that Jeff hated every minute of their jeers and threats, although most of the time he didn't say a word. As the days passed, his anxiety grew and so did his anger. I tried to convince the other inmates to let up so Jeff would know I was someone he could talk to and trust. More than anything, I wanted him to listen when I spoke about the word of God and how Jesus Christ provides the answers to all our problems.

I prayed that his tortured soul would find peace in the knowledge that Jesus Christ died on the cross for our sins . . . for all of our sins, even his.

Thirteen
Is Your Soul Dead?

"Simon, Simon, Satan has asked to have you, to sift you like wheat, but I have pleaded in prayer for you that your faith should not completely fail. So when you have repented and turned to me again, strengthen and build up the faith of your brothers." Simon said, "Lord, I am ready to go to jail with you, and even to die with you." (Luke 22:31-33, TLB)

Wednesday, March 4, 1992.

We were *still* on lockdown. Some inmates on our tier had ninety minutes of recreation three times a week. Dahmer, however, had to remain in his cell. I could have gone to recreation that day but didn't want to.

As the inmates returned, they slowed at Dahmer's cell and it was the same old thing–abusive, threatening language hurled at him. I don't know how Jeff could stand it every day. Abusive words filled with hate were something I couldn't tolerate, regardless if they were aimed at me or at someone else.

Mail call at 11 a.m. was more of the same, hundreds of letters for Dahmer. Since he could only have twenty-five in his cell at a time, he probably only saw one-tenth of his mail. Officers let him scan the envelopes and choose those he wanted to read.

At noon, I heard an officer talking to Jeff about his mail.

"Who writes to you, anyway?" I asked after the officer left, thinking about the piles of letters that went unopened.

"Various people from all over the country," he replied. "I get a lot of mail from people in Canada, Germany, Great Britain, and Africa, too."

"Do they ask you questions?"

"They ask me things like, 'How did you cook the human flesh?' and 'Did you use any seasoning?'" he said, amused. "Some also tell me they think I got a raw deal. Some ask about prison, 'What's in your cell?' and others merely want my autograph.

"I get a lot of mail from white-supremacist groups such as the Ku Klux Klan, the Aryan Brotherhood, and the Skinheads. I also get letters from women who send me their pictures. Some of them ask me to marry them from prison. Can you believe that? I don't even bother to answer most letters."

I began wondering if Jeff thought he was a normal, sane person. Did he realize that he had a problem? At the time, I knew my answer to that question, but I wondered what *he* thought.

I asked Jeff, point-blank, "Do you think you're suffering from a mental illness?"

"I'm just as sane as the next person," he casually responded. "I knew exactly what I was doing then and now."

"But why did you do it, do all of it?" I asked, speaking about the murders. What Jeff did went *beyond* just killing people; it was ritualistic, sadistic, and more than strange.

He didn't respond.

Remembering what he had said on a previous day, about how he didn't understand why I was talking to him about God, I asked, "Do you think your soul is dead?"

Jeff remained silent. Perhaps he was really thinking about what I had asked. Finally, he said, "After my first killing in Ohio, I started drinking heavily. I knew then that my spiritual soul had died. At times, I felt nothing. At other times I felt like a time bomb of destruction."

I didn't know what to say. Jeff, no doubt, suffered from so much pain that he couldn't understand it, deal with it, rationalize it, or likely even feel it. It was as if he had gone numb and empty, pushing God, and good, out and letting Satan in.

At 4:30 p.m., we had supper. After each meal when officers collected the trays, they gave Dahmer his medication as usual. He always had to open his mouth, showing the officer he swallowed the pills.

After supper, we could shower, but Jeff declined. I think he was still afraid of the other prisoners. He didn't want to give them any additional opportunity to berate him.

As I passed his cell, I saw that he was reading his letters with his glasses on, animatedly chewing gum. Reading letters and chewing gum . . . that was the extent of his life in prison. At least the letters gave him something to do, but they probably didn't make him feel any better. I'm sure they only reminded him of the awful things he had done. Of course, there's a good chance that he liked being reminded about what he had done.

I remember thinking about my own situation. Sometimes I'd get depressed and brood about how I could be in prison for ten years and how dark and dismal my future looked. Then I'd think about Jeff's situation–his crimes and fifteen consecutive life sentences with no hope of parole, ever. When I compared his life to mine, I always felt better.

During and after showers that night, the inmates started again with their threats and jokes. Jeff never said a word in response to them. His silence made the guys mad, so they'd yell angry, vile curse words.

Jeff still didn't respond.

When things finally got quiet that night, Jeff and I again talked through the air vents.

I asked Jeff why he decorated the bedroom wall in his apartment with skeleton drawings and photos.

"Well, I couldn't exactly have the full skeletons of my victims hanging around," he said, "so I had pictures. I'd fantasize that the pictures were pictures of all my victims. I'd look at them and masturbate."

My disbelief never seemed to wear off; I couldn't get used to his answers. His new responses shocked me just as much as the ones prior. He didn't have any remorse at all; nothing in his words suggested that he felt what he did was wrong.

As usual, I didn't let my shock stop my curiosity. I asked him about eating human flesh. He said he really only did that one time. He told me how he ate part of the biceps of one of his victims. He had tried to eat it raw at first. "It had a rough, salty taste and it wasn't very pleasing because it was tough. Cooked, it was better."

That comment made me sick. I tried not to get visuals in my head about all the things Jeff told me, but it was sometimes unavoidable. As our time together continued, I still had no appetite. Many times food, especially meat, looked *really* unappetizing. I made a mental note never to ask Jeff questions about his crimes around mealtime.

Once again I told Jeff to read the ninth chapter of Matthew, about how Jesus delivered the people of the country of the Gadarenes who were possessed by devils. I had just told him to read that same verse the day before but I wanted him to read it again because I felt it was something important that Dahmer should read, remember, and try to understand.

A herd of pigs was feeding in the distance, so the demons begged, "If you cast us out, send us into that herd of pigs." "All right," Jesus told them. "Begone." And they came out of the men and entered the pigs, and the whole herd rushed over a cliff and drowned in the water below. (Matthew 9:30-32, *TLB*)

Then I told him that the Bible said that demons are organized into a body of people, classified according to rank or authority, like a military command.

There were times during our conversations that Jeff told me he did accept the Lord as his savior. I wanted to believe him, but I just wasn't sure if he understood the power of God's love and forgiveness. I wondered if Jeff really believed he could be forgiven for his sins.

That night, after sitting and thinking for quite awhile, I wrote Jeff a letter. I tried to get my feelings about his soul and his need for redemption on paper. I believed I could organize my thoughts more clearly and explain it better on paper than I could while standing on a sink, talking through air vents.

I kept the first draft of the letter I wrote that night and mailed the good copy to Jeff through the prison mail system. Here's what the letter said:

Hello Jeff.

First of all, I pray to God that you are doing OK. It's good to always remember that God has always looked out for me by keeping in touch with good Christian people. Jeff, the scripture of Isaiah 61:1 says, "The spirit of the Lord God is upon me, because the Lord hath anointed me to preach good tidings unto the meek. He hath sent me to bind up the broken-hearted, to proclaim liberty to the captives, and the opening of the prison to them that are bound."

I told you that I will constantly write you and encourage you to stay on the Lord's side, because knowing him as your personal savior is all that we would ever need in our lives. So brother, I am praying that when you start to follow Jesus, there's no turning back.

Please! Jeff, constantly read your Bible when Satan tries to come in your immediate thoughts. When he tries to take your joy, don't give him the opportunity. You are a born-again Christian and the day you decided to follow God was the best decision you could ever make. Leaning on God's understanding will strengthen your belief. Jeff, both of us know that our Heavenly Father can do more than we can ever imagine. So I am ending this letter by saying, prayer can change things.

Your brother forever, Calvin.

I signed my letters Calvin because I was using the name Calvin Earl Martin when I was arrested, and it was the name I kept using in prison.

Later that night the third-shift officer picked up the letter and some Christian literature for Jeff. I also filled out a request form asking to speak with the chaplain about my case. I wanted to ask him for his special prayers and encouragement.

I felt good about the conversation I had with Jeff. I was glad I wrote the letter and eager to hear his response. I drifted off to sleep, another day in solitary confinement over.

Fourteen
More Questions, More Answers

When he comes back he will take these dying bodies of ours and change them into glorious bodies like his own, using the same mighty power that he will use to conquer all else everywhere. (Philippians 3:21, TLB*)*

Thursday, March 5, 1992.

Same old story–breakfast, medication, shaving equipment, mail call. Jeff hit the wall, indicating he received my letter and literature.

Even though the amount of mail Jeff was receiving had finally started to taper off, he still got bags of it daily. He told me some of the letters coming now were death threats.

I told Jeff that even Charles Manson, imprisoned since 1969, still received letters from strangers, alleged followers, and, of course, people who hated him. I figured Jeff would get letters for the rest of his life.

After lunch, he told me one of the letters he got that day said the author admitted wanting to be just like him. Jeff chuckled, but I didn't say anything. The thought was bone chilling.

That evening, Pastor Dawson came to talk to me about the request form I sent to him. I explained my situation with the razor blade found in my old cell and I reiterated that it wasn't mine.

Pastor Dawson told me to tell the truth. "God knows what's in your heart. He knows if you're guilty or not. You'll be OK if you always tell the truth." Then he prayed with me, right there outside my cell.

As the chaplain was leaving, he stopped at Jeff's cell and chatted with him for a few minutes.

Later that night, while everyone was resting and watching TV and it was quiet, Jeff and I began our usual discussion. Trying to satisfy my endless curiosity about his crimes, I asked him how he met his victims. I also asked him how he got those men to so willingly return to his apartment on their own.

"I met them at the common places any person would go to meet people: bars, parks, malls, Laundromats, bus stops," he said. "I'd promise them the sexual experience of a lifetime or sometimes I'd tell them I had drugs or money that I would give them. I told them I had large quantities of whatever they desired at my apartment and that they could have all they wanted if they came with me."

Like any good con man, he told them what they wanted to hear. I imagine it was hard for most of Jeff's victims to resist. Many of his victims had criminal records; few had jobs. They were all looking for something and often Dahmer appeared to have just what they thought they needed: drugs, sex, money, or a combination of the three. Sometimes I wondered if that was all Jeff did, even now: tell people what he thought they wanted to hear.

One of the things I had always been curious about was the victim he had tried to turn into a zombie. What could he have possibly been thinking when he drilled a hole into young Konerak Sinthasomphone's head, and dripped acid into his brain? Did he honestly think that was a viable option and was that *really* his intent? There was only one way to find out. "Were you really trying to create a zombie who would serve your every need, like a slave?" I asked.

The words seemed strange coming from my mouth. The question bothered me because I already knew the answer would be equally as disturbing as my question felt.

"Anything's possible, isn't it?" Dahmer answered. "We're taught that while we're growing up. We're taught that we can be whatever we want to be, so why couldn't I control people? It didn't hurt to try. The act of doing it was completely erotic, actually." It was half of an answer.

I told Jeff to look in his Bible in Ephesians and read what the Apostle Paul had to say about our battle with Satan.

For we are not fighting against people made of flesh and blood, but against persons without bodies–the evil rulers of the unseen world, those mighty satanic beings and great evil princes of darkness who rule this world; and against huge numbers of wicked spirits in the spirit world. So use every piece of God's armor to resist the enemy whenever he attacks, and when it is all over, you will still be standing up. (Ephesians 6:12-13, *TLB*)

Jeff said something like, "Yeah, I guess I need God's armor, all right. I need something."

I knew Jeff wanted to hear more, so I said a prayer that God would show me which verses in the Bible I should share with him that night. Psalms came to mind.

For the Lord is a great God, the great King of all gods. (Psalms 95:3, *TLB*)

I wanted Jeff to understand that there was no place for Satan in his life. He had to accept God as king.

Jeff was silent, so I started making some notes. I wrote down words: Satan, sin, faith, love, commandments, witnesses, discipleship, prophecy, salvation. I figured if I could take Jeff step by step from Satan to salvation, then I'd be getting somewhere. I knew I could not *personally* save Jeff. All I could do was give him the tools, show him the way, and encourage him. He still had to take it upon himself to learn, try, and believe.

So we began.

"Jeff, look up I Peter 5:8. It says, 'Be careful—watch out for attacks from Satan, your great enemy. He prowls around like a hungry, roaring lion, looking for some victim to tear apart.'

"Don't you see, Jeff, that's what you were doing? Looking for victims. You were doing Satan's work for him."

Jeff mumbled. "Yeah, I guess. You really think Satan can take control of a person's mind?"

"Of course! He had you, man! Look up James 1:15. This one's about sin. It says, 'These evil thoughts lead to evil actions and afterward to the death penalty from God.' You hear that, Jeff? You didn't get the death penalty 'cause Wisconsin doesn't have a death penalty, but in God's eyes you did. And that's why you have to ask his forgiveness sincerely, to wipe out that sin, just like the death of his son wiped out our sins for us. You get it, man?"

"So God forgives even murder, huh?" Was I making progress or was he being snide?

"Yup. Even murder; even many murders. OK. Next, let's talk about faith. It's important. Look in Hebrews 11:1. 'What is faith? It is the confident assurance that something we want is going to happen. It is the certainty that what we hope for is waiting for us, even though we cannot see it up ahead.' All you need is faith, man. Faith. It's a special gift, but you gotta have it."

"How do you get it?" Jeff asked.

"You just believe. Believe with all your heart and soul and mind. You just know that God is there for you, because he is. He really is. Then, the next thing comes love. It all just falls into place. Love. I John 4:7. Read it, Jeff. 'Dear friends, let us practice loving each other, for love comes from God and those who are loving and kind show that they are the children of God, and that they are getting to know him better.' That's what you're doing, Jeff, you're getting to know God better and better. And once you get to know the love God has for you, it's very easy to love other people. Don't you see? It spreads like a virus. Love. It's all that matters."

I was happier by the minute as the pieces seemingly fell into place. We were on a roll and Bible verses were coming to me right and left.

Next, we talked about the commandments.

"Jeff, read the whole chapter of Exodus 20. That's where you'll find God's commandments."

I was quiet while Jeff read. I was sure he'd probably studied the Ten Commandments at some point during his childhood, but I doubted that he'd reviewed them lately.

"Now you know about God's laws. OK, now let's go up to Proverbs 14:25. That's where it says we have to be witnesses to the Lord. It's not enough to just know and obey the commandments. We also have to tell others about God."

A witness who tells the truth saves good men from being sentenced to death, but a false witness is a traitor. (Proverbs 14:25, *TLB*)

After that, we talked about discipleship and how God would honor those who honor him by sharing the good news of God with others. I often prayed that Jeff would have it in his heart to eventually open up to some of the other prisoners and become a disciple on his own.

If these Greeks want to be my disciples, tell them to come and follow me, for my servants must be where I am. And if they follow me, the Father will honor them. (John 12:26, *TLB*)

The last two things I wanted to talk to Jeff about that night were prophecy and salvation. The first, prophecy, was the answer to why all these Bible verses happened to come to me that night. They were the perfect verses for what I was trying to share with Jeff.

I knew it wasn't me; it was the Holy Spirit acting through me, using me as a conduit to spread the Word. It says so right there in 2 Peter 1:21. "For no prophecy recorded in Scripture was ever thought up by the prophet himself. It was the Holy Spirit within these godly men who gave them true messages from God."

I read that to Jeff so he would know that even here in our cells at Columbia, the Holy Spirit resided with us.

Our night of sharing ended with a powerful verse from Acts about salvation. Once again, I asked Jeff to read his Bible along with me while I read the verse aloud.

There is salvation in no one else! Under all heaven there is no other name for men to call upon to save them. (Acts 4:12, *TLB*)

He was quiet, so I spoke up. "Look Jeff, the most important thing here, and the whole point of all this, is for you to accept God into your heart, to see and to understand the sins you committed. You have to be sorry for what you did wrong. You can't ask for forgiveness if you're not truly sorry.

"God can see into your heart. He knows if you're faking and are only going through the motions in an attempt to achieve salvation. It's like when Jesus condemns the hypocrites in Matthew 6:5-6."

I paused for a moment hoping Jeff would look it up, but I didn't hear him flip any pages. Suddenly, I felt tired and drained so I didn't look it up either. I remembered this verse well because Levy used it to explain how important it was not to be a hypocrite.

I summed it up for Jeff.

"Jeff, the hypocrites Jesus talks about are the people who act pious and holy on the outside, but aren't truly like that on the inside. They have a false relationship with God." I waited.

"Yeah," Jeff whispered, barely audible.

I felt like maybe Jeff was overwhelmed or sad. He didn't say anything more. It was late. My brain was tired of thinking and my hand was tired of writing. Each night as we talked, I would write everything Jeff said in my journal. Of course, he didn't know I was doing that. Though it was innocent and with the best intentions, if he had known I was documenting our conversations he probably would have stopped talking to me.

At times when I couldn't write fast enough, I'd ask him to repeat himself, saying other inmates were too loud and I hadn't heard what he said. In reality, I just wanted to write it all down so I wouldn't forget. By writing it down, I could reread it and plan which Bible verses I would share with him the next night.

We had developed a pattern. I'd get him talking by asking something about his crimes, try to relate what he did to Satan's control over him, and then take him step by step through God's plan toward salvation. I just hoped it was all making sense to him. I wanted so much for this tortured man to understand that he could break away from evil.

I wanted him to know that he could find happiness again, if he would only open his heart to the goodness of the Almighty. I believed that with all my heart. I just wasn't sure Jeff did.

Before I closed my eyes I said, "Jeff, the spirit of God reveals things to you. Keep an open mind. The spirit will come, just you wait."

Fifteen
Inferiority Complexes

Soon a Samaritan woman came to draw water, and Jesus asked her for a drink. He was alone at the time as his disciples had gone into the village to buy some food. The woman was surprised that a Jew would ask a "despised Samaritan" for anything—usually they wouldn't even speak to them!—and she remarked about this to Jesus. He replied, "If you only knew what a wonderful gift God has for you, and who I am, you would ask me for some living water!" (John 4:7-10, TLB)

March 6, 1992.

After breakfast, shaving, and standing count, the inmates on Desegregation Unit 2 had recreation. Once again, I didn't feel like going outside just to stand around or pace in a fenced cage. Jeffrey didn't either.

At the 11 a.m. mail call, Jeff got his usual bags of mail to sort through and choose the twenty-five letters he wanted to read. That day I also got a letter—from Jeff. He must have sent it the previous day. Jeff told me he also tried to send me some books, but security wouldn't approve.

Jeff's letter said it was hard for him to know who to trust and that he was glad to be writing to *someone* who didn't hate him for his crimes.

"I'm glad to hear that you're a Christian," his letter went on to say. "I've just started to read the Bible, so I have a lot to learn about the Lord Jesus Christ and how to live the Christian life. It's great to know that the Lord Jesus loves us enough to save us from our sins! Like you said, when it's all said and done, knowing Jesus as your Lord and Savior is all that really matters."

He ended by saying, "Yours thru Jesus Christ our Lord. J.D.," adding, "You're right, we all come short of the glory*!*"

After I read the letter, I slapped the wall so Jeff would know I was talking to him.

Inferiority Complexes

"Jeff, I got your letter. Hey man, it makes me happy to hear you're trying to find some spirituality in your life. You can find happiness with the Lord, even here in prison."

After lunch, my advocate, who was a social worker for inmates housed on Units 8 and 9, came to talk to me about the conduct report concerning the razor blade incident and about my confinement. He told me my hearing would be the following week, on Wednesday, March 11. I'd be appearing in front of the whole committee.

That afternoon I thought a lot about what might happen at that meeting. If found guilty, I'd be transferred to Desegregation Unit 1 for a rehabilitative and adjustment program for whatever amount of time the committee suggested, probably somewhere around six months.

After the advocate left, Jeff asked, "Calvin, why are you over here in DS-2, anyway? What'd you do?"

"Security found a razor blade in my cell on Housing Unit 2," I told him. "It wasn't mine, though. I didn't put it in the window. Besides, I don't have any enemies here at CCI and that's my main defense. I don't need a shank weapon here, so why would I have one stashed? It had to have been the guy in the cell before me that put it there. I just gotta prove it to the committee next week so I can get out of here."

After supper, I filled out a form requesting that one of my teachers at the prison school be my character witness at the hearing.

After the 9 p.m. standing count, armed with my pad of paper and pencils, I started asking Jeff more questions. I had to hit the wall between our cells quite hard to get his attention. He must have been sleeping, but I finally heard him mutter.

I was blunt. "Jeff, can I ask you something? Are you a racist?"

He answered right away. "Yeah, I guess I am. I've proven my superiority over non-whites with the crimes I've committed. What I did proves that whites are the highest form of life on this planet."

I paused. I felt so sorry for him, to have these thoughts and feelings inside him. I thought about Jeff's first victim, Steven Hicks, who was white and died in 1978 in Ohio when Jeff was only seventeen years old.

"Why did you end up killing that kid, Steven Hicks?" I asked. "Why did you want to do it?" That boy hadn't been a minority, so it couldn't have been racially motivated.

"I don't know, I guess it was an experiment of some kind. I wanted to see what it felt like to kill someone."

It was such an awful thing to say. He killed a person *just because he wanted to try it.* He stole someone else's life, ruined a family, all because he was selfish and sick. But for some reason I began to think maybe Jeff wasn't telling me everything; maybe it was deeper than that.

"If you hadn't gotten caught, would you still be doing the same thing?" I asked him. "Would you still be killing?"

"Definitely," he said without hesitation. "I'd have lots more victims. Yes. I would've killed and killed until I either achieved my goal of an all-white America or got caught. I knew I'd be getting caught sooner or later, although I believed it would have been much later than it was."

"Didn't you care at all about your victims, no matter what color they were?" I asked.

"To be honest, I didn't give a fuck about them. You don't understand, you never killed anyone, but I actually enjoyed it while I was doing it. I drugged 'em all first, so they didn't feel anything. They didn't know what was happening. I just enjoyed the power of being in control of their bodies."

"Why did you drug them so they wouldn't feel any pain? If you were going to kill them anyway, what difference did it make?" I asked.

"Because when they were drugged, I could get them to do anything I wanted without them struggling. It was easier and more enjoyable."

I didn't say anything, mainly because I was busy writing. I didn't know what to say anyway. I felt sad because it seemed that even after all our talks about God and forgiveness, he was still just as hateful and unremorseful as before. I wanted to talk about Jesus and the Bible, but I wasn't as prepared as I'd been the in the past.

I couldn't figure Jeff out. Sometimes he would seem like a changed man, interested in God and being a good person, but then there would be moments like these when the serial killer emerged all over again.

Jeff started talking again, this time about his probation officer, Donna Chester. On May 23, 1989, under terms of his probation, she was to meet with him every week.

"She was an idiot," Jeff said. "I hope her eyes are open now."

I asked him about Gerald Boyle, his attorney. I wanted to know how he liked him and if they got along.

"I don't think he could stand me," he said, "just like most people couldn't. At least he did his job. I don't care what other people think about me."

Then Jeff started talking about how he also resented his parents and his childhood. He talked about how his parents rarely spent time with him, which was why he hung out in the woods so much. That was where he got interested in cutting up dead animals. He was alone all the time and his fantasies were open to run wild because no one was there to guide him in other directions.

"We [he and his parents] argued all the time when I was a teenager. I hated it," he said.

Jeff said he was really upset when his parents divorced and when his dad married Shari. He said he was angriest when his dad made him enlist in the Army after he flunked out of college.

"He did it just to avoid spending time with me," he said. "I know that. He wanted to spend more time with her [Shari]."

I asked one more question. I couldn't determine if he was *truly* racist or hid behind racism. "Why did you target multiracial men … blacks, Indians, Hispanics, Asians?"

"I guess because I was picked on as a child. I'd just go into those clubs and I'd just want to pick on somebody who wasn't like me. I never liked any of those other races."

I didn't quite understand what he meant. It was as if he still tried using racism as an excuse. His reasoning didn't make sense to me.

Neither of us said anything for awhile; then he said, "Do you ever wonder why God caused Negros to be black and dumb or illiterate?"

I couldn't let myself get angry or say anything back. He was probably trying to push my buttons, so I tried to change the conversation into something positive. I started thinking about what it said in the Bible about prejudice. I remembered a verse in Acts about treating everyone equally, so I looked it up.

"Jeff, will you open your Bible to Acts, Chapter 10? It's the story about a Roman officer named Cornelius. He was a godly man and respected by the Jews. An angel appeared to Cornelius and told him to send for Simon Peter, who was Jesus' right-hand man. The angel said Peter would tell Cornelius what God wanted him to do with his life. When Peter came to Cornelius' home that evening, the Roman soldier fell on the ground to worship Peter."

I started reading the verses from my Bible, hoping Jeff was following along.

But Peter said, "Stand up! I'm not a god!" So he got up and they talked together for awhile and then went in where the others were assembled. Peter told them, "You know it is against the Jewish laws for me to come into the Gentile home like this. But God has shown me in a vision that I should never think of anyone as inferior." (Acts 10:26-28, *TLB*)

Jeff said he always thought God catered to one race, the white race.

"But that's not true, man. Just remember that verse, 'God has shown me in a vision that I should never think of anyone as inferior.' We are all equal in God's eyes. Nobody's inferior."

Jeff was quiet after that. I asked him a few more questions but he wouldn't respond, so I stopped. We both had lots to think about that night.

Sixteen
The Pull Between Good and Evil

One of them, a lawyer, spoke up: "Sir, which is the most important command in the laws of Moses?" Jesus replied, " 'Love the Lord your God with all your heart, soul, and mind.' This is the first and greatest commandment. The second most important is similar: 'Love your neighbor as much as you love yourself.' All the other commandments and all the demands of the prophets stem from these two laws and are fulfilled if you obey them. Keep only these and you will find that you are obeying all the others." (Matthew 22:36-40, TLB)

Saturday, March 7, 1992.

The first weekend in Unit 2 was my worst time in prison. There was no recreation; nothing to do except sit in my cell. Neither Jeff nor I had visitors or appointments.

The 11 a.m. mail call brought more bags of mail for Jeff. He figured he was getting about a thousand letters a week.

"How do you decide what mail to read?" I asked him.

"I look where it's from, which city, state, or country; then pick the ones with the most interesting-sounding names. Or I read the ones with designs on the envelopes or the ones with colored envelopes."

Every afternoon that week, new prisoners came to our unit for different violations. Every time a new prisoner arrived, he joined the "let's ridicule Dahmer" group.

That night after supper, the jokes started in on schedule. Most weren't even funny.

Finally, after standing count that night, things got quiet and I pulled out my pad of paper.

I asked my neighbor, "What were some other ways that you got black guys to come back to your apartment, especially because you are a white guy?"

"It was easy," Jeffrey replied. "If I saw anyone looking at me at the various bars, I'd start talking to them. Sometimes I'd say, 'Do I know you?' Or, 'Have we met some other place before?' You know, the usual tactics, small talk. When we got to my apartment, I'd tell them that the apartment belonged to a black friend of mine who's in the Army and he had to report back to the base. Then I'd say that my black friend said I could keep the apartment until the rent ran out. I figured they'd feel more comfortable there if they thought it belonged to a black man. That way, being with a white guy wouldn't seem so weird to them."

"Didn't your neighbors suspect anything?" I asked. "What about loud noises?"

"I always made up some story about the noises when I was using the saw or drills, something about remodeling. They complained about the smells, so I'd make up something about that–cleaning fluids or whatever."

"If you had lived in an area that was mostly white, instead of a black neighborhood, would this killing spree have gone on so long?"

"If I only killed whites, it would have ended a long time ago," he said. "That's one reason I targeted minorities. Whites are superior. The families would have been more outraged if the victims were all white. They would have been reported missing right away and stuff like that."

His answer was sad and frustrating. It reminded me of that Laotian boy who had escaped Jeff's apartment only to be escorted back by the police. There was a lot of outrage regarding how the cops handled that situation; many believed racism was the reason the boy was returned to Jeff. Was he right? Was there some logic behind his rationale?

Jeff continued, cutting off my thoughts. "Another reason I chose blacks is that they were easier to trick once they saw my money. If I promised them money, they'd come to my apartment easily."

I didn't counter his answer but instead asked him, "How do you feel about the victims' families? What would you like to tell them now?"

Jeff must have been in a lousy mood that day because he said, "The simple fact is that I don't give a fuck about them or how they feel. I knew each of the victims had families when I killed them, and I also knew that I would cause them a lot of pain in doing what I did, but I didn't care. I really don't have any remorse for what I did. I do regret getting caught, more should die, but it's over for me. I would like to say to the families that I truly enjoyed what I did and that I regret nothing."

Jeff's words upset me so much I could hardly talk. How could anybody be so cold, have no conscience or empathy or sorrow? The more I thought about it, the less I believed that Jeff really meant what he said. In fact, the more I talked to Jeff over the next few days, the more I was convinced he didn't mean a lot of what he said, especially about not regretting his actions.

Up to now, Jeff sat in his cell with nothing to do except read. Some letter writers wrote saying what he did was good; other wrote and threatened him, wishing he would die. He had to be confused just reading those letters and listening to the ridicule coming from the other inmates on our tier. Nobody in the tier said anything nice to him except me.

He seemed to fear leaving his cell, even for recreation, so I could imagine he said those hateful things out of frustration. I think comments that he made were more than just lashing out; I believe he tried to blend in and sound like a cold-hearted tough guy.

I reread the letter he sent me and realized there was an internal struggle going on inside him. One minute he was letting Jesus win, the next he was letting Satan win. I honestly didn't think what was coming out of his mouth was what was actually in his heart.

"Jeff, how do you feel about what the media had to say about your crimes?" I asked.

"I believe the majority of [the media] didn't get the picture of *why* I did what I did. They wrote what they believed and it's all fucking lies. They can think what they want, but it doesn't matter because they're just as confused about me and my actions as the public is, so fuck them."

I'd never seen or heard Jeff this defensive or agitated. Again, I thought his constant confinement was getting to him. I said people were curious about him, and the media reported what they knew and got their stories from different sources. It was true; no one in the media had interviewed Dahmer so, beyond the police reports, everything was hearsay.

I wanted to comfort him. He seemed so upset and angry, so tormented. Maybe he didn't understand what he did or why he did it. Maybe hatred and racism was an excuse, not a motive at all. Perhaps it was just easier and made more sense to him to say those vulgar things. I didn't know how to feel about it, but I wasn't going to give up on him.

I asked Jeff to open his Bible to the Book of Daniel, Chapter 10. I read a verse to him that talked about how Daniel was afraid. I suspected Jeff was afraid, maybe so terrified about what would happen to his soul that at times, he just gave up and let the hatred and evil emerge when he talked.

I read the verse aloud:

Then he said, "Don't be frightened, Daniel, for your request has been heard in heaven and was answered the very first day you began to fast before the Lord and pray for understanding; that very day I was sent here to meet you." (Daniel 10:12, *TLB*)

I told Jeff, "Demons can do various things to Christians such as take control over the person's mind, body, and spirit. As long as Jesus is on the throne of the believer's heart, no demon can reside there. But the temptations are always there to slip back into our old ways of thinking and that's when the demons can cause believers a great deal of torment. If we invite a demon in, he will come in. He'll move into our minds and tempt us and deceive us. I think what you said earlier tonight were the words of a demon."

That night I wrote Jeff another letter and sent it along with a Christian magazine and some scriptures. Here's what I wrote:

My dearest brother Jeff,

Just as I sat down here to write to you, God put it in my heart to read from John, Chapters 13 and 14.

"And so I am giving a new commandment to you now—love each other just as much as I love you. Your strong love for each other will prove to the world that you are my disciples." (John 13:34-35, *TLB*)

"If you love me, obey me; and I will ask the Father and he will give you another Comforter, and he will never leave you." (John 14:15-16, *TLB*)

"The one who obeys me is the one who loves me; and because he loves me, my Father will love him; and I will too, and I will reveal myself to him." (John 14:21, *TLB*)

"Judas (not Judas Iscariot, but his other disciple with that name) said to him, 'Sir, why are you going to reveal yourself only to us disciples and not to the world at large?' Jesus replied, 'Because I will only reveal myself to those who love me and obey me. The Father will love them too, and we will come to them and live with them. Anyone who doesn't obey me doesn't love me. And remember, I am not making up this answer to your question! It is the answer given by the Father who sent me." *(*John 14:22-24, *TLB)*

My dear friend, we must love each other. Love comes from God, and when we love each other, it shows that we have been given new life. We are now God's children, and we know HIM.

Jeff, GOD is love, and anyone who doesn't love others has never known HIM …

GOD showed his love for us when he sent his only SON into the world to give us LIFE …

REAL love is not our love for GOD, but his love for us.

GOD sent his SON to be the sacrifice by which our SINS are forgiven.

Brother Jeff, those scriptures were put in my mind to share with you.

Your Christian Brother,

Calvin

After I finished that letter, I wondered what else I could do to help pull Jeff's soul away from the devil and into the arms of God our Savior. All I could do at that moment was pray, pray unceasingly, like it says in the Bible. And so I did.

I didn't sleep well that night. Awful thoughts found their way into my head. I was worried about Wednesday's hearing. I worried about my future, too. Jeff came to mind often. Sometimes I believed he had filled my head with nightmares, all those things that he told me, all those terrible things he did. I wanted Jeff to find God. I knew God was the only answer.

Seventeen
A Quiet, Lonely Sunday

The first time I was brought before the judge no one was here to help me. Everyone had run away. I hope that they will not be blamed for it. But the Lord stood with me and gave me the opportunity to boldly preach a whole sermon for all the world to hear. And he saved me from being thrown to the lions. Yes, and the Lord will always deliver me from all evil and will bring me into his heavenly kingdom. To God be the glory forever and ever. Amen. (II Timothy 4:16-18, TLB)

Sunday, March 8, 1992.

Sundays were as quiet as Saturdays, and just as boring; nothing to do and no outside mail. Jeff received the letter I wrote him along with the magazines and literature.

Quite a few prisoners had visits from friends and family, but not me. Not Jeff, either.

On that particular Sunday evening, inmates in the regular housing units attended church services in the chapel between 6:30 and 8:30 p.m., but not those in Unit 2. I didn't like missing church services. In fact, I was starting to hate this restricted unit. Time passed far too slowly.

On the other hand, I knew God put me there for a reason. So even though I was tired, I pulled out my Bible to find verses to share with Jeff that night.

After the 9 p.m. standing count, I tapped the wall to get his attention. I always tried to say something interesting to get him talking before I started asking him questions.

I wanted to know more about his probation officer. It seemed like he didn't want to talk about her much. In fact, he just repeated the same things he'd said the night before and then dropped the subject.

I asked him about the police officers who brought Konerak Sinthasomphone, the fourteen-year-old Laotian boy, back to his apartment in May 1991.

"I thought for sure I was caught," Jeff said, "and I was even more shocked when the officers left him with me without even asking to look in my bedroom. They'd have been surprised to see three bodies in there, wouldn't they? That just shows you how ignorant society is on this planet. Those officers had no idea whether they were doing the right thing or not. I still can't believe they handled the situation the way they did."

"What about your parents, Jeff?" I asked. "How do you feel about them now and what did you think about them before?"

Jeff thought for a moment, then answered cautiously. "They were good at one time, but they became blind, like most people on this planet, to the fact that we must rid this earth of scums. I love my parents, but I have no pity for them. It's up to them to open their eyes to the facts themselves."

I didn't really understand what Jeff was talking about but I had a feeling he was going to go off on one of his racist rants again. I didn't want to hear it.

I didn't feel like talking to him anymore and I couldn't think of any more questions so I opened my Bible and started reading, looking for more scriptures that might help him.

A little while later, I said, "Jeff, do you know that our Lord, Jesus, the son of God, has complete authority over demons?"

I wanted to make sure Jeff knew that God is the all-powerful one, not Satan. I also wanted two things specifically: I wanted him to be free and I wanted him to be a better person. I prayed to God that He help me find the right words to say. I wished I could have gone to church to pray about it.

I ended that dreary, lonely Sunday by telling Jeff to read the following scriptures: Matthew 16:17-19, Ephesians 6:10-11, I John 4:4, and Hebrews 2:14-15.

Even though we couldn't attend church and worship God as part of a group, at least I hoped Jeff would end that Sunday by reading his Bible. Since I wasn't sure if he would or not, I decided to read the verses aloud. I tried to read slowly so he could understand what I was saying. I prayed he would listen closely and really hear the words, then think about them later.

A Quiet, Lonely Sunday

"God has blessed you, Simon, son of Jonah," Jesus said, "for my Father in heaven has personally revealed this to you–this is not from any human source. You are Peter, a stone; and upon this rock I will build my church; and all the powers of hell shall not prevail against it. And I will give you the keys of the Kingdom of Heaven; whatever doors you lock on earth shall be locked in heaven; and whatever doors you open on earth shall be open in heaven!" (Matthew 16:17-19, *TLB*)

"Imagine that, Jeff. Jesus is giving you the keys to heaven. But you have to open those doors to forgiveness, first, and then the Lord will let you into heaven. You can do that, Jeff. All you have to do is ask forgiveness."

He didn't answer. Maybe he was asleep, I don't really know. I was always afraid that the drugs he took made him sleep too much. I kept reading, just in case.

Last of all I want to remind you that your strength must come from the Lord's mighty power within you. Put on all of God's armor so that you will be able to stand safe against all strategies and tricks of Satan. (Ephesians 6:10-11, *TLB*)

Dear young friends, you belong to God and have already won your fight with those who are against Christ, because there is someone in your hearts who is stronger than any evil teacher in this wicked world. (I John 4:4, *TLB*)

"Jeff, you hear that? There is someone in your heart who is stronger than any evil in this wicked world! That someone is God, Jeff. You know, I've been feeling bad today. It was a long day. I'm tired of being here. I'm worried about that razor blade hearing coming up. I'm sick of worrying about everything. Jeff, are you listening to me? Here's the bottom line: We both need to know that nothing is going to happen to you or to me that you and I can't handle. Isn't that right? It's true, if we have Jesus on our side, we can handle anything! Jeff, listen to this:

Since we, God's children, are human beings—made of flesh and blood—he became flesh and blood too by being born in human form; for only as a human being could he die and in dying break the power of the devil who had the power of death. Only in that way could he deliver those who through fear of death have been living all their lives as slaves to constant dread. (Hebrews 2:14-15, *TLB*)

I didn't hear anything from Cell 1. I felt a mixture of sadness and determination surrounding Jeff. I had so much passion in me to help him; the words of God burst from my lips but seemed to go unheard and unseen by the closed ears and eyes in Cell 1. I felt like falling to my knees in exasperation and pounding my fists against the thick cement wall separating us. I wanted Jeff to see and to understand, but he seemed so lost. In Jeff's case, he probably never really saw or understood God. God was never a part of his life, and now it seemed like a distant world.

I tried to imagine what Jeff was thinking. He probably felt like the Lord had abandoned him a long time ago, so now he would abandon God in return. If only he could see how much God loves and how God was with him right then trying to save His troubled child.

I fell asleep amidst prayers that my scripture readings would touch Jeff's heart and that we could talk about them the next day. At least the next day would be Monday and the long, long weekend would be over.

Eighteen
Another Letter from Jeff

Don't be fooled by those who try to excuse these sins, for the terrible wrath of God is upon all those who do them. Don't even associate with such people. For though once your heart was full of darkness, now it is full of light from the Lord, and your behavior should show it! Because of this light within you, you should do only what is good and right and true. (Ephesians 5:6-9, TLB)

Monday, March 9, 1992.

Once again, when offered the chance to go outside for some fresh air, Jeff didn't go. Neither did I.

At 11 a.m., the mail came and Jeff got his usual bags and bags of greetings from people all over the world. That day someone even sent him a nineteen-inch color television set, but he couldn't keep it because it was equipped with a built-in clock timer, which was not allowed. He sent it back.

I received another letter from Jeff, which he wrote the previous night. He thanked me for the magazine. He said that some nights he was so bored he wished he could go to sleep and never wake up. He complained about having to write with a marker because apparently the guards were afraid he'd stab himself if they gave him a pen. He also talked about missing the club scene in Chicago on Saturday nights.

"Have you ever seen Chicago at night? All the buildings are lit up; it's nice," he said.

He ended by telling me to keep my spirits up and he'd try to do the same.

I read the letter, then tapped the wall between our cells.

"Hey, Jeff, I got your letter. Thanks."

"No problem," he said. "I tried to send you some books again but security wouldn't let me. I don't know why. They're just books."

"I understand." I didn't really, but I said it anyway. I was curious about what types of books he had planned to send to me. What type of book did Jeffrey Dahmer read or, for that matter, what kind of book did he want *me* to read?

Jeff interrupted my thoughts.

"Hey, Calvin, do you go to Chicago very often?"

"No, hardly ever," I admitted.

"Well, I loved it. The nightlife and the lights, they're the best in Chicago. I'd take the train or the bus. That's where I met some of my victims. They'd come back to Milwaukee with me on the bus and I'd take them to my apartment. We'd spend the whole weekend making love, but then, when they were ready to go back to Chicago, I'd have to drug 'em so they wouldn't leave. You know the rest."

I did know the rest. I knew it pretty well by now and appreciated his lack of elaboration.

That Monday was the first and only day I remember that Jeff came out of his cell to take a shower. He was out of those four walls for about ten minutes. He just had to walk a few feet because his cell was across the hall from the shower area. None of the other prisoners could see that he was out of his cell except me.

After the 9 p.m. standing count, I asked Jeff how he felt about his life sentences. I couldn't imagine what it would be like knowing I'd never get out of prison.

"It's true," Jeff sighed. "I'll be locked up forever, for as long as I live. But the thoughts and fears of what I did will be immortal. It's my legacy. What I did will be written in books and will be with people for time eternal. I can only hope it will be used by the right individuals to achieve the same purpose as I tried to achieve."

Jeff's answer sounded like it was something he had thought a lot about; like it was a speech he had prepared and knew well. I didn't have a response. I often felt at a loss for words when I was talking to Jeff. He was a complicated guy and I never quite knew what to expect from him.

Then, changing the subject, he asked, "I have a question for you, Calvin. Do you think, when you get out of prison, you'll still stay a Christian?"

I was thrown by his question, but answered. "Yes, of course I will."

"Do you think it will be hard, you know, staying with God and all?"

"Man, life is hard and it's full of temptation," I replied. "Satan is always there trying to pull you away and make you go down a bad path. But that's what being a Christian is all about, staying with God even when times are hard."

Jeff was silent, so I continued, "God will always be there, but it's up to us to have faith and turn to Him when we are in trouble."

I was glad that Jeff wanted to know more about Christianity. He was such a different person at night. I began to wonder how he could be so sarcastic and evil-minded during the day and yet so willing to learn about God and the Bible at night? It was strange and confusing, but I thought maybe his disrespect was an act to get back at the other inmates for all the jokes and threats. Maybe he figured he was giving them what they wanted to hear, what they expected of him.

I started to think that maybe Jeff knew prison was the best place for him. It was where he felt safe and where he belonged, where he couldn't hurt any more people.

My mind wandered and I began thinking about Jeff's trial. "Jeff, what do you think about the judge who sentenced you? Judge Gram?"

"He did what he had to do just as I did what I had to do," Jeff replied. "I feel no anger toward him. Just by my trial he should have realized that all minorities should die and I hope I've made that impression on him."

"How about Attorney Gerald Boyle? Did you like him?"

"I believe he did his job and nothing more," Jeff said. "I know he couldn't stand me as most people can't, but I'm not bothered by what people think or I wouldn't have confessed to all the crimes I committed."

It was time for our two-man Bible study. I quietly reviewed what I had planned for that evening.

Then I told Jeff, "God's final plan for Satan and his demons is found in Matthew 25:41. Read it. It'll help you in your spiritual walk."

Then I will turn to those on my left and say, "Away with you, you cursed ones, into the eternal fire prepared for the devil and his demons." (Matthew 25:41, *TLB)*

"Jeff, you sure don't want to spend eternity in hell with the devil and his demons, do you?"

Jeff responded casually. "I don't think I'm afraid of dying. Not anymore." He paused for a moment and then continued, "I think it would be the best thing for me actually. Besides, I would probably fit right in with the demons and the devil. We'd probably be pals."

Jeff was being sarcastic. I knew he didn't mean what he said. Maybe he wasn't afraid of death anymore because he probably already felt dead; his life was over as far as he was concerned.

I was quiet as I tried to find the right thing to say.

"Jeff, you can't give up on living." I ignored his comment about being pals with the devil. "There is still so much good you can do with this life you were given. Your soul can still be saved."

I didn't hear an answer, so I figured he was asleep. I tried to stay positive but it was difficult.

I looked up Psalms 23 in my Bible and read it quietly to myself. This verse always made me feel better. Even I sometimes needed a reminder that God was with me during my most troubling times. Living next to Jeffrey Dahmer was a challenge. Trying to get him to know and love God was even more of a challenge and that challenge had started to get to me.

I wondered if he would ever have a change of heart big enough to sincerely ask for God's forgiveness. Was all my work with him for nothing? Would this mass murdering serial killer eventually come around to the Lord? I prayed about it and then I finally slept.

Nineteen
The Day Before My Disciplinary Hearing

Don't be fooled by those who try to excuse these sins, for the terrible wrath of God is upon all those who do them. Don't even associate with such people. For though once your heart was full of darkness, now it is full of light from the Lord, and your behavior should show it! Because of this light within you, you should do only what is good and right and true. (Ephesians 5:6-9, TLB)

Tuesday, March 10, 1992.

Three things kept my mind occupied during the days in Unit 2. I thought maybe God had placed me in that cell because he knew I was a relatively new Christian and, therefore, was as far as introducing him to the power of God and all the excited about my faith. I wondered if I was doing enough with Jeff as far as introducing him to the power of God and all the goodness that awaited him if he would only believe that Jesus was his Lord and Savior.

My hearing also occupied my thoughts. I worried a lot, especially about what would happen if I was found guilty.

The third thing I thought about was leaving the desegregation unit, getting back with the general prison population where I would have more freedom; where I would be able to continue my classes, attend chapel services and Bible study, go to the gym, library; and where I could talk to the friends I'd made in prison. I hated being cooped up in one cell all day and all night but on the other side of the story, I would be away from Jeff. My thoughts contradicted themselves. I wanted to be out of this timeless unit but I also felt I had a responsibility to keep talking to Jeff about God.

It felt like each day in Unit 2 lasted more like three days. The boredom was broken a little on that day when I received a memo in the morning mail.

Date: March 9, 1992

To: Calvin Martin, #139891

          DS-2, Cell 2

From: Captain Pete Huibregtse

Subject: TLU Status

This is in response to your correspondence to Mr. Davidson dated 030692. You will remain in TLU status pending the outcome of your hearing. An investigation will not be ordered at this time unless determined necessary by the hearing committee.

I was hoping officials would do an investigation before the next day's hearing so there would be proof that I hadn't hidden that razor blade, but deep down I knew they wouldn't. I couldn't eat that night because I was so nervous.

Luckily, the other inmates on our tier were quiet for once and didn't start with their usual Dahmer bashing. I was glad. It gave me more time to think about my immediate future.

After the 9 p.m. standing count, I thought that no matter what happened the next day, I probably wouldn't be in Unit 2 any longer. If found guilty, I'd be doing adjustment time on Unit 1. If found not guilty, I'd leave Unit 2 and return to a different cell in another unit, possibly my former cell. I knew this night could be my last chance to talk to Dahmer.

Even though I wasn't feeling good and my mind was heavily preoccupied, I decided to ask him more questions. I also had a few more Bible quotes I wanted him to read. I went over and pulled myself up onto my sink. I balanced myself and tapped the wall.

"Hey, Jeff, tell me what you think, honestly. Do you think you'll go to heaven after all you've done?" I hoped Jeff felt differently today. It was a new day and every day was a new beginning with new opportunities to make life better.

Dahmer, without much hesitation, answered, "I know what I said the other night, about going to hell. And I thought about it and I wondered, 'why would I not go to heaven?' Yes. Basically, I believe what I did was right. Somebody has to rid the earth of scum. Why would I be punished for that? If I am punished, it'll be by making me continue to live on this earth, knowing that scum like that are still walking around freely, contaminating this planet and its people. That's torture right there, having to stay on this earth."

I was stunned and frustrated; sometimes it felt like Jeff would take one step forward but then take *ten* steps back. Just the other day he said he was probably going to hell and hinted that he realized what he had done was wrong. He must be angry or bitter today.

I honestly believed that deep inside his troubled soul, he was sorry for his crimes, but for some reason he felt he had to randomly shock me with his weird theories and racial slurs. I'd read in the newspaper about what Dahmer had told the judge the day he was sentenced. He had said then that he wanted to take back the awful things that he did. He even apologized to the families and said he was sorry for all the pain he had caused them.

Why was he being so hateful about his victims now? He couldn't seem to make up his mind about how he felt about things, or what he wanted to tell people. He seemed so confused.

Almost every night we had a conversation and it was usually the same routine. Maybe it was because Jeff had figured out that I was a black man and he knew mostly black men in the other cells ridiculed, threatened, and joked about him. Perhaps talking to me like that was his way of getting back at those men who hated him.

At any rate, because I felt that Satan himself still tormented Jeff, I wanted him to read more scripture that warned us about Satan and how he tried to control the world and each of us who are tempted to do evil.

I sat on my bed and paged through my Bible, looking for the verses I had in mind. Finally, I had a list to read to Jeff.

"Jeff, write these verses down and read them tonight: II Corinthians 2:10-11, John 6:37 and 40, Romans 8:35-39, and II Thessalonians 3:3.

"Yeah, OK. I'll read 'em." I could hear Jeff scribbling down the verses and the two of us were quiet for some time. All I could hope was that he was in that cell, behind that concrete block wall, reading the verses with an open mind.

When you forgive anyone, I do too. And whatever I have forgiven (to the extent that this affected me too) has been by Christ's authority, and for your good. A further reason for forgiveness is to keep from being outsmarted by Satan; for we know what he is trying to do. (II Corinthians 2:10-11, *TLB*)

But some will come to me–those the Father has given me–and I will never, never reject them.

For it is my Father's will that everyone who sees his Son and believes in him should have eternal life–that I should raise him at the Last Day. (John 6: 37 and 40, *TLB*)

Who then can ever keep Christ's love from us? When we have trouble or calamity, when we are hunted down or destroyed, is it because he doesn't love us anymore? And if we are hungry, or penniless, or in danger, or threatened with death, has God deserted us? No, for the Scriptures tell us that for his sake we must be ready to face death at every moment of the day–we are like sheep awaiting slaughter; but despite all this, overwhelming victory is ours through Christ who loved us enough to die for us.

For I am convinced that nothing can ever separate us from his love. Death can't, and life can't. The angels won't, and all the powers of hell itself cannot keep God's love away. Our fears for today, our worries about tomorrow, or where we are–high above the sky, or in the deepest ocean–nothing will ever be able to separate us from the love of God demonstrated by our Lord Jesus Christ when he died for us. (Romans 8:35-39, *TLB*)

But the Lord is faithful; he will make you strong and guard you from satanic attacks of every kind. (II Thessalonians 3:3, *TLB*)

I especially wanted Jeff to read and study the verses from Romans because they offered hope to every sinner in the world. I wanted Jeff to know that the power of God's forgiveness was limitless. I wanted him to find peace in the power of God's ultimate love. Nobody could love anyone greater than God. I believed that and I wanted Jeff to feel God's unconditional love. I wanted him to reach out and touch the hand of God and to become one of his children.

Twenty
Hearing Day Arrives

Stand steady, and don't be afraid of suffering for the Lord. Bring others to Christ. Leave nothing undone that you ought to do. I say this because I won't be around to help you very much longer. My time has almost run out. (II Timothy 4:5-6, TLB)

Wednesday, March 11, 1992.

After breakfast and shaving, we could go outside for recreation for twenty minutes. As usual, neither Jeff nor I attended recreation. I'm not sure why Jeff never wanted to go outside, but on that day, I was too nervous about that afternoon's conduct hearing.

I told Jeff about my hearing. We talked about what I could get as far as additional time if I was found guilty. He wished me luck and said he hoped everything came out OK.

Jeff's usual bags of mail arrived and, just as they had done every day, security spent hours sorting the letters on large tables down the hall.

Around 1:30 p.m., two officers came to get me for my hearing. They shackled my feet, cuffed my hands, and escorted me to the hearing room in Desegregation Unit 1. The room looked just like a small courtroom.

The two officers stood guard during the proceedings. Also present were the captain, unit manager, the officer who found the razor blade in my cell, and the social worker who was my math teacher and character witness.

I sat down, shaking because I was so nervous. I lowered my head and prayed silently to myself. *Please, Lord, be with all of us today, and let the truth come out. I have faith that the truth will set me free. Praise you, God. Amen.*

After the officials read the charges against me I told my side of the story.

"I use Magic Shaving cream," I said, "and I buy thirteen-cent disposable razors at the canteen. I don't even use that brand of blade. I didn't know the razor blade was in the window.

"I haven't had any problems with security since I came here. I haven't had many conduct reports in my whole life."

I didn't want to sound desperate or scattered, but my words spilled out faster than I could control them. I was innocent.

"Besides," I continued, "the warden told us he would be doing searches. Because I didn't have anything to hide, I didn't even worry about it. I didn't even bother to clean my cell because I wasn't worried about the searches. I don't have any enemies here, so why would I even want a blade like that?"

I received a copy of the "Record of Witness Testimony" report, signed by one of my teachers, Bruce Tulpa. Mr. Tulpa wrote, "I have no personal knowledge of the conduct report. Calvin is an excellent student. Above expectations. No problems with other inmates or in class."

Also on that same sheet was Officer Hoffman's report about finding the razor blade. He wrote, "The item was a razor blade removed from a razor. Had tape across the back side of the razor–fully left the razor's edge exposed. Found in upper right-hand corner of the screen, partially stuck in the sealer of the screen. A person could have gotten the razor out with a paper clip. Nothing else was found of any type from that razor."

I felt sick and nervous but tried to focus on remaining calm. I prayed again.

Committee members discussed the evidence and my testimony, and then voted "not guilty" on all three charges. On the written report titled, "Disciplinary Hearing: Reasons for Decision and Evidence Relied On," dated March 11, 1992, which security gave me later that day, it simply said, "Charges do not substantiate a finding of guilt. Dismissed."

I was so happy; I let out a huge sigh of relief. God answered my prayers.

The relief I felt was incredible. I thought about that poem, *Footprints in the Sand*, where the man learns that in the times of greatest stress and hardship, instead of walking beside him, God actually carried him in his arms. I felt that was exactly what happened to me. All I could say when it was finished was, "Thank you, Jesus. Thank you. Praise God. Thank you, Jesus." I said it over and over as officers escorted me back to my cell.

I returned to gather my things. Finally, I could leave the restricted area.

While I was packing, I told Jeff that things had gone well for me, that all the charges were dropped, and that I was being moved to a different unit.

"Praise God," Jeff said. "I'm happy for you, man."

I added a few "praise God's" of my own and, as I gathered up my things, I told Jeff that I'd keep writing letters to him. I couldn't resist asking him a few more questions before I left.

"Tell me, Jeff, did you honestly have sex with those men and boys after they died?"

"Yes."

"What drove you to do that?"

"Desire, I guess."

"How many did you have sex with?"

"Roughly most."

I shook my head, still finding it hard to believe that this man I had befriended in the cell next to me had committed such monstrous crimes.

"Well, Jeff, take care of yourself. And don't forget to read your Bible every day. I hope you read all those verses I gave you. I'll be writing you from wherever they send me. So long."

"Yeah, Calvin. You take care."

I had mixed feelings about leaving Jeff. I was extremely happy to be out of the desegregation unit and on my way to better things. At the same time, I felt sad for Jeff and, in a way, I was going to miss him. I prayed that he would keep God in his heart and do what he could to make the best of his future. I hoped he would let go of his demons and try to live in a new light.

I knew I had done all I could to help Jeff. I could only hope that Jeff used the tools I gave him to help himself. It was up to him now, but I would continue to write and offer encouragement.

Around 3 p.m., I arrived back at my old cell, Cell 35 in Unit 2. My buddies were glad to see me and I was glad to see them. It felt good to be back where things were somewhat normal.

"Hey, Calvin, you look like you lost weight," one of my friends said.

"I did," I said, thinking about the gruesome stories Dahmer told me that killed my appetite.

"Calvin, man, you only been gone a few weeks. You couldn't eat?" I knew they were curious about what happened to me while I was away.

I told them where I was, that I lived in the cell next to Dahmer, that I talked to Jeff about his crimes.

"Hell, no. I had a lot on my mind. I was nervous about my hearing, plus hearing some of Dahmer's stories got to be a bit much at times. I lost my appetite a lot." For the first time I laughed a little while thinking about it.

My time with Jeff already started to feel like a lifetime ago. It was nice to be back.

A few days later, I sent Jeff a letter and a Christian card that I got from the chapel. I wrote a note on the card telling him to be sure to stay with God. Here's what I wrote:

May today be a blessing, Jeff. It has been awhile since we spoke or saw one another and, just as I said previously, I would continue assisting you with knowing our Lord Jesus.

First I want to share with you something I have learned through studying the Word. It's related to some of the things from the Bible and what the Bible stands for and means. Since you want to live for God, here is what the word Bible means:

B – Bibliographical

I – Internal Harmony

B – Bible Prophecy

L – Lord's View

E – External Evidence

Also, Jeff, the word FAITH stands for:

F – Forsake

A – And

I – I

T – Trust

H – Him

So, brother, that's all good for you. Please read these scriptures to assist you with your walk with the Lord: II Timothy 3:16, II Peter 1:16, Hebrews 1:1-2, John 3:18, and Mark 13:31.

Well, Brother Jeff, I am ending this letter and my prayers are with you.

Brothers of Christ,

Calvin E. Martin

The whole Bible was given to us by inspiration from God and is useful to teach us what is true and to make us realize what is wrong in our lives; it straightens us out and helps us do what is right. (II Timothy 3:16, *TLB*)

For we have not been telling you fairy tales when we explained to you the power of our Lord Jesus Christ and his coming again. My own eyes have seen his splendor and his glory. (II Peter 1:16, *TLB*)

Long ago God spoke in many different ways to our fathers through the prophets [in visions, dreams, and even face to face], telling them little by little about his plans. But now in these days, he has spoken to us through his Son to whom he has given everything, and through whom he made the world and everything there is. (Hebrews 1:1-2, *TLB*)

There is no eternal doom awaiting those who trust him to save them. But those who don't trust him have already been tried and condemned for not believing in the only Son of God. (John 3:18, *TLB*)

Hearing Day Arrives

Heaven and earth shall disappear, but my words stand sure forever. (Mark 13:31, *TLB*)

The next week, sometime between March 15 and March 19, I heard on the radio that Jeff had returned to Desegregation Unit 1 after he was caught trying to confiscate a razor blade.

Security must have given Jeff a razor, but when security received his razor back, he had removed the blade. The officers found the blade wrapped in a tissue in his wastebasket. Jeff knew inmates weren't supposed to take the blades out of the razors, so I earnestly believe he was up to something.

I thought about all the other inmates on the unit who had been threatening him day after day and wondered if Jeff's life was filled with so much fear that he'd kept that blade as security. The thought also crossed my mind that he was filled with so much despair, that he was thinking about ending his own life.

I was sad that day. More than anything, I cared about Jeff's soul. I wanted him to live for Jesus, because for Jeff, that's all he could do. Being with Jesus was all he had to look forward to and I didn't want him to forsake that.

I wondered what he was doing, what he was thinking or feeling. I prayed that Jeff would stay strong.

Twenty-One
Corresponding with Jeff from Afar

Turn from all known sin and spend your time in doing good. Try to live in peace with everyone; work hard at it. For the eyes of the Lord are intently watching all who live good lives, and he gives attention when they cry to him. (Psalms 34:14-15, TLB)

As soon as the security officer noticed the blade missing from Dahmer's razor, other officers arrived at his cell. They handcuffed Jeffrey, opened his door, and told him to step out of his cell.

Security searched everything inside the cell and one officer found the blade hidden in the plastic trash basket. Jeff returned to the glass tank in Desegregation Unit 1.

The officer who found the blade wrote up a report stating Dahmer tried to conceal the blade in his trash basket. All three offenses that were on my conduct report were now on Jeff's: damage or alteration of property; possession, manufacture, and alteration of a possible weapon; and possession of contraband, miscellaneous.

If Dahmer had asked for a due-process hearing, he could have called fellow inmates, staff members, or officers as witnesses. If he requested it, Jeff would have gone through everything I did with my razor-blade incident, but he didn't bother. Even though the media knew of Dahmer's razor-blade incident, the whole thing blew over in a few days.

Things at Columbia returned to normal for the next few months . . . with one exception: I was no longer there.

On Monday, March 23, 1992, at 8:30 a.m., I was transferred to the Racine Correctional Institution in Sturtevant, Wisconsin. The Racine facility is a medium/maximum-security institution.

I didn't lose contact with Jeff, however. Nor was I kept in the dark about what was going on at Columbia. I learned that my friend Mark was in my old cell next to Dahmer's. Mark wrote and told me the Columbia gossip. I wondered if Mark ever talked to Dahmer and, if he did, I wondered what they discussed. A few of my friends who were swampers at Columbia also transferred to Racine and gladly shared what they'd seen and heard about Jeff during the course of their jobs.

I learned that after a month or so in the glass tank, Jeff spent the month of May and part of June back in Cell 1. Mark said they gave Jeff a TV, radio, and a fan during those hot months, which was more than the other prisoners got. He said the officers also let him go into the dayroom where he could watch TV by himself or make phone calls. He was always alone.

In the meantime, I attended church services every week at the Racine institution. Pastor Tommy Thomas was a rehabilitated ex-con who gave up a life of crime and drugs. I liked Pastor Tommy because he was somebody with whom I could identify.

I also continued my classes in school and, often in the evenings, I'd write to Jeff.

The next time I wrote to Jeff, I thought about all the mail he received and how he chose just twenty-five letters a day to read. I was determined, with God's assistance, that he would choose my letter. In that particular letter, I wrote about Paul's struggle as described in Romans 7:15-25. I copied those verses in the letter so Jeff wouldn't have to look them up.

I don't understand myself at all, for I really want to do what is right, but I can't. I do what I don't want to—what I hate. I know perfectly well that what I am doing is wrong, and my bad conscience proves that I agree with these laws I am breaking. But I can't help myself, because I'm no longer doing it. It is sin inside me that is stronger than I am that makes me do these evil things. I know I am rotten through and through so far as my old sinful nature is concerned. No matter which way I turn I can't make myself do right. I want to but I can't. When

I want to do good, I don't; and when I try not to do wrong, I do it anyway. Now if I am doing what I don't want to, it is plain where the trouble is: sin still has me in its evil grasp.

It seems to be a fact of life that when I want to do what is right, I inevitably do what is wrong. I love to do God's will so far as my new nature is concerned, but there is something else deep within me, in my lower nature, that is at war with my mind and wins the fight and makes me a slave to the sin that is still within me. In my mind I want to be God's willing servant but instead I find myself still enslaved to sin. So you see how it is: my new life tells me to do right, but the old nature that is still inside me loves to sin. Oh, what a terrible predicament I'm in! Who will free me from my slavery to this deadly lower nature? Thank God! It has been done by Jesus Christ our Lord. He has set me free. (Romans 7:15-25, *TLB*)

After I wrote out that verse, I explained to Jeff that Paul was talking about bondage, about control of the power of sin. I wrote: "Jeff, Jesus set us free! His promise is right there in Romans 8:2. 'For the power of his life-giving Spirit—and this power is mine through Christ Jesus—has freed me from the vicious circle of sin and death.' Jeff, the scripture teaches us that when Jesus died on the cross, our old sinful ways died with him. Jeff, don't dwell on the things in your past, your old sins. Instead, rejoice in being free now from that vicious circle of sin and death. Free! That's God's promise."

I closed my letter by reminding Jeff that we no longer had to be slaves of sin. "Read Romans 6:6 and try to remember it. Read it every day, Jeff. It says, 'Your old evil desires were nailed to the cross with him; that part of you that loves to sin was crushed and fatally wounded, so that your sin-loving body is no longer under sin's control, no longer needs to be a slave to sin.' Jeff, keep your mind on salvation.

"You kept that razor blade to do what Satan had in mind. You let down your guard. Think only of God and how he sent his only son to save us. Keep your guard up. Set your mind every day on the spirit of God. Satan lives to put us into bondage. But God lives to free us. Just remember that."

Corresponding with Jeff from Afar

I didn't hear from Jeff for awhile, but that didn't mean I didn't hear *about* him.

In May 1992, Jeff went to Ohio to stand trial for the 1978 murder of Steven Hicks, his first victim. In Ohio, Jeff plead guilty. The Ohio judge again sentenced him to life, which brought his total consecutive life sentences to sixteen.

In August, Jeff began taking Prozac. His mood had brightened and he seemed more animated. He was no longer entirely segregated from other prisoners and he talked about getting a job. Jeff complained that he had too much time on his hands and wanted a job as a custodial worker.

He began work as a part-time janitor in his unit.

We heard that an anonymous benefactor had donated money to Jeff's prison account and, with it, had bought a dozen or so books. The books were about creationism and evolution. To me, it sounded like Jeff was trying to figure out the meaning of life.

At the end of August, Jeff wrote to me, addressing me as "Brother Calvin." He mentioned how happy he was to receive my letter, and that he was glad to hear I was still reading the Bible. He went on to say, "I feel that the most important thing in life is to accept the Lord Jesus Christ as Lord and Savior. I'm glad you did! Because you accepted him as your Lord and Savior, He will give you a future in heaven better than anything you can imagine!"

He ended by telling me to "Keep trusting in our great Lord and Savior, Jesus Christ."

On the envelope of that letter was a sticker that said, "Compliments of J.D. The name of the Lord is a strong tower; the righteous run to it and are safe. Proverbs 18:10"

I answered Jeff's letter. I told him to read Romans 5:10. "And since, when we were his enemies, we were brought back to God by the death of his Son, what blessings he must have for us now that we are his friends, and he is living within us!"

I encouraged Jeff to be positive in his fight against Satan and to rejoice in having Jesus Christ now living inside him. I was so happy. Jeff really seemed to be turning around. I hoped he finally realized the error of his ways and was sincerely sorry for the pain he caused.

Just a week later, in September 1992, I received another letter from Jeff. Again, he called me "Brother Calvin." He spoke about being transferred from Cell 2 to the SMURF unit and said he spent most of his time reading and watching TV. He was excited about a new cable station, TNT.

He said he was still getting some mail, but much less than he had in the beginning, although the letters still came from all over the world. He mentioned Africa, Australia, Germany, Ireland, Wales, Canada, Spain, and England. He hadn't answered many letters because he thought his handwriting was bad, but he guessed he might write back more if he got a typewriter. He told me his birth date, May 21, 1960, and ended by telling me to keep reading my Bible.

He included two photocopied pages from an article called, "How You Can Enjoy Superb Health," with the letter. There was a list of food do's and don'ts . . . pretty weird stuff.

In October 1992, Jeff moved to a private cell in Unit 6, west side, bottom floor, close to the officer's booth. It was a better unit where he had more freedom to move. Even though he was on a more relaxed unit, he remained under heavy supervision as well as under continued observation by the unit psychiatrist and psychologist.

Around that time he took a different job. This position consisted of cleaning the dayroom and cleaning cells when inmates moved to another unit, another institution, or were released.

Word trickled back to Racine that television shows such as *A Current Affair* and *Inside Edition* sent Dahmer books and magazines.

Even after he moved into Unit 6, Jeff stayed to himself. He drank a lot of coffee, smoked cigarettes, and didn't talk to many people. My friend, Mark, told me in a letter that people still sent Dahmer bags and bags of mail and gifts. Once he received so many Bibles that he donated fifty to the Columbia Correctional

Chapel. Some people sent household items and cookware for him to autograph and send back. Of course he didn't do this. In fact, Jeff had to return or give away most items.

One officer said Dahmer received lots of jewelry and clothing. He kept some of the clothing but sent most of it to charitable organizations.

About the only notable thing that happened in December 1992 was that Jeff's grandmother died. I wondered if he ever felt badly about how his crimes affected his family. It must have been difficult for his family to live normally after the discovery of Jeff's crimes.

In January 1993, an officer at Racine said Dahmer stopped reading most of his letters because he believed people were trying to take advantage of him. Jeff's father took many of the letters back to Ohio when he came for his monthly visit.

Sometime during that same month, I made the mistake of telling Jeff in a letter that I wanted to write about him. He never corresponded with me again.

I didn't give up on him, however, and continued to write him week after week the whole time I was at Racine. At that point, all I could do was hope he read my letters from the hundreds he received each week.

In general, I believed Jeff's life got better the longer he spent in prison.

By spring of 1993, Jeff weighed somewhere between 210 and 225 pounds, had a beard, and wore his hair cut short. Too much eating and too little exercise had caught up with him. I also thought since he wanted to get out of his cell more, maybe he felt the need to disguise himself from the other prisoners. He probably didn't want to listen to more threats or jokes.

By this time, Jeff was eating his meals with the other inmates in the cafeteria. He also attended recreation in the gym or library with the other inmates on Units 6 and 7. He, like all the other prisoners, could smoke in the dayroom during indoor recreation, outside during recreation, or in his cell. At that time, Jeff told some staff members that he still had too much time on his hands. He wanted to work more outside his cell. He said he needed a job with more hours and he'd heard that a position in the gym was available.

Jeff got the job and began work as a custodian, mopping, waxing, and buffing floors in the gym along with other general cleaning. He worked from 7:30 until 11 a.m. five days a week for seventeen cents an hour. After the first month, he would have been making twenty-eight cents an hour, with the possibility of earning up to thirty-three cents an hour.

Each day an officer escorted him to and from the gym. The officer would search him before leaving his cell and before returning to his cell.

Jeff participated in recreational activities such as weightlifting, basketball, and horseshoes. He started jogging around the half-mile track once a week, too.

During that year, Jeff had his own group of inmates whom he talked to or played cards with at times. He attended Wednesday evening Catholic religion services occasionally. I was happy to hear that he was still making the effort to learn and gain an understanding of God's goodness. No one was forcing him attend those services; he was doing that all on his own.

Jeff bought a lot of junk food from the canteen. Generally, by the summer of 1993, he acted like any normal prisoner, although he was still a quiet man who stayed to himself.

Jeff's mother, Joyce Flint, who was now living in Fresno, California, finally began to visit her son in the summer of 1993. Other than infrequent visits from his family and attorneys, we never heard that anyone else ever visited Jeff.

Despite his seemingly ordinary life on the inside, there still were some areas where Jeff dared not go. Whenever the institution had a big gathering such as a cookout, Jeff never attended.

One guy told me that Jeff learned to crochet in the hobby room and crocheted blankets and other things.

Whenever he had to sign anything, he'd just write "Jeff" and nothing more. He started painting pictures in the hobby room and even sold signed paintings. Hard to say what, if any, of this information was true because we heard it through the prison grapevine.

One correctional officer who worked at Columbia said Jeff was meeting expectations at the institution. It was a blanket statement, but probably not too far from the truth.

Twenty-Two
Unanswered Letters

How beautiful upon the mountains are the feet of those who bring the happy news of peace and salvation, the news that the God of Israel reigns. (Isaiah 52:7, TLB*)*

Whenever an inmate arrived at Racine from Columbia, I always asked about Jeff. Sometimes they'd tell us about the other inmates on Jeff's unit who continued to threaten him. I felt sorry for him and wanted to encourage him to keep with Christ. One thing I knew was that Dahmer desperately needed God in his life. Although I was so glad to be out of Columbia and out of solitary confinement, sometimes I wished I could be there for Jeff: reading him scriptures, giving him someone to talk to, and teaching him about the ways of being a Christian.

I continued to write to Jeff and encouraged him with his religion and his Bible study. I knew he needed lots of support, so I sent him cards that I got from the chapel.

At various times I'd send Christian literature to help Jeff fend off an attack from Satan. A verse from Ephesians kept coming back to me. Paul wrote to the Ephesians to warn them, just as I wrote to Jeff to warn him.

As I said, Jeff never wrote to me again, but I sincerely hoped he read my letters. I wanted to help him and knew that if he opened his heart to God, his life would be better. I sent my letters anyway, always telling him about the word of God and offering support no matter how hard things got.

In one letter I said, "Jeff, in Ephesians, Chapter 6, verse 10, it says, 'Last of all I want to remind you that your strength must come from the Lord's mighty power within you. Put on all of God's armor so that you will be able to stand safe against all strategies and tricks of Satan.' "

Verse 13 says what I tried to say to Jeff in every letter I wrote: "So use every piece of God's armor to resist the enemy whenever he attacks, and when it is all over, you will still be standing up."

I also told him not to let the other inmates bother him. It was Satan testing him, trying to make him turn away from God. I reminded him about the *Footprints in the Sand* story, telling him that even in our most troubled times, the Lord is still with us. I also told him to think about better things and to try to find interests or hobbies to keep him occupied. It appeared Jeff was taking interest in new things. I knew it would help him and make him a better person. For me, when I started taking classes and learning new things, I truly felt happier, and regardless of my sentence, I felt optimistic toward life. I tried things I never thought I could do.

The next week I wrote another letter. I told Jeff that salvation meant deliverance. If God's grace saved us, we would be delivered into heaven. It was as simple as that.

I explained that early in Jesus' ministry, he visited the synagogue in his hometown of Nazareth. During the service, he stood up and quoted from a prophetic passage in the Old Testament, Isaiah. Jesus wanted the people in that synagogue to understand that he was the fulfillment of that prophecy.

The spirit of the Lord God is upon me, because the Lord has anointed me to bring good news to the suffering and afflicted. He has sent me to comfort the broken-hearted, to announce liberty to captives and to open the eyes of the blind. He has sent me to tell those who mourn that the time of God's favor to them has come, and the day of his wrath to their enemies. (Isaiah 61:1-2, *TLB*)

I wanted so much for Jeff to keep the hope in God no matter what. I knew that if that hope died within him, the power of Satan would rise again and he wouldn't have the strength to continue his study of Christianity. Even in prison, Jeff had to keep his soul alive with hope, hope that eventually he would be reunited with God in heaven.

A couple of weeks later I wrote another letter.

Jeff,

If Jesus could unleash the poor from the chains of poverty, free the prisoners and deliver the blind from their infirmity, imagine what good things come to those of us who are also saved by the goodness of Jesus! When we say that we've been saved, we mean that we've been set free from the penalty of our sins. It's true that the Bible says, "the wages of sin is death." But Jesus' death on the cross paid that price for each one of us. Brother Jeff, when we put our faith in Jesus, we are delivered from condemnation instantly and eternally. That is a salvation Satan can never take from us and it's our greatest defense against his attacks.

Jeff, once we become Christians, there are still things from which we must be set free. We must be set free from affliction and Satan and his demons. Don't you know that it was Satan who made you keep that razor blade in your cell? He is trying to debilitate you, brother. But just remember, God has given you salvation. You can trust him to set you free from other afflictions that Satan puts before you.

Another time, I told him about how God saved David. David, who wrote seventy-three of the Psalms, wrote many of them during personal times of tragedy. I asked Jeff to read Psalms 34:4, 6, and 18.

For I cried to him and he answered me! He freed me from all my fears. (Psalms 34:4, *TLB*)

This poor man cried to the Lord–and the Lord heard him and saved him out of his troubles. (Psalms 34:6, *TLB*)

The Lord is close to those whose hearts are breaking; he rescues those who are humbly sorry for their sins. (Psalms 34:18, *TLB*)

In that same letter I told Jeff one more time that he should not be anxious about anything, that we simply have to let our requests be known to God and the peace of God will guard our hearts and minds. With that peace, we can overcome the circumstances of our lives. I reminded Jeff that Jesus Christ would strengthen him to live out his days in peace and contentment if he would just put his faith in the Lord.

I said, "Jeff, your circumstances, fears, troubles, broken-heartedness, illness ... those things do not have to control you. You only need call on the Lord, have faith in his deliverance and you will be given the strength of Jesus himself."

When I mailed that letter, I prayed that Jeff still had his faith in God and that he would receive my words in his heart with an open mind.

Another time I recalled Psalms 91:11-12. This was one of my favorite passages in the Bible because it offers such hope for a safe life on the outside.

For he orders his angels to protect you wherever you go. They will steady you with their hands to keep you from stumbling against the rocks on the trail. (*TLB*)

I knew that when I got out of prison that God's angels would protect me and keep me from stumbling against the rocks of life. I just hoped that in prison, Jeff would find the same comfort.

These many ideas, feelings, scripture quotes, and beliefs about God and his son, Jesus Christ, which I shared with Jeff, came to me from many sources during the years since I had become a Christian. Various volunteers, chaplains, pastors, and Christian brothers all worked with me at different times and places. One thing they taught me was that I would never know enough about the goodness of the Lord. My quest to learn more about God and his goodness should never end.

In addition to trying to help Jeffrey find a sense of peace by committing his life and his soul to God, I was going through hard times of my own. Each time when I felt depressed about my life, I automatically picked up my Bible and started reading. Before long I started to feel better, hopeful. I learned that without hope, we can't go on, but with the hope that God gives us so generously we can do anything, go anywhere.

One day I wrote a letter to Pastor Gene Dawson at the Columbia Correctional Institution. I discussed my faith and how I was trying to stay with God, to be positive. I also asked him how Jeff was doing. Pastor Dawson wrote back.

July 22, 1993

Dear Calvin Martin,

It was good to hear from you. I am pleased to hear you are remaining faithful to our Lord Jesus Christ.

Remember, to grow in our spiritual life, it is very important that we 1) read the Holy Bible, study the Holy Bible (II Timothy 3:16-17); 2) pray daily (James 5:16, Psalms 34:15, Proverbs 15:29); 3) develop friendships with Christian brothers and sisters (Hebrews 10:25); 4) get involved in Christian service (II Thessalonians 3:13, Galatians 6:9, Matthew 28:18-20, Acts 1:8, Matthew 22:37).

In answering your questions about Mr. Jeffrey Dahmer, I can only say he has been very generous in donating many books to the Chapel, and seems to have it together. He has not been to Chapel for several months. It certainly is appropriate to remember him in your prayers, as well as the other men here at CCI that they too would come to the saving knowledge of Jesus Christ as their Lord and above all, their Savior.

Thanks for your letter. Perhaps I will see you sometime very soon as a free man.

Very Sincerely,

Gene Dawson

Chaplain CCI

I was grateful for that letter from the pastor. After I read it, I didn't feel so alone. It felt good to receive some spiritual support. I was also glad to hear about Jeff, to know that for the most part he was doing OK.

As the days and weeks and months ticked by in Racine, I often thought about why God placed me, a new Christian, in the cell next to Jeffrey Dahmer's.

133

I knew that my excitement in finding the hope that Jesus gave helped me talk to that man whose soul I honestly believed Satan inhabited.

I believe it was God's will and the work of the angels that I live near Jeff so my Christianity could rub off onto him. God gave me a special gift, the opportunity to share God's goodness with a sinner so confused by Satan that he became one of history's worst criminals. I believed with all my heart that God wanted me to share with Jeff the message of hope that I had received just a few years before.

It's a message I continue to share.

Twenty-Three
My Release from Prison

Keep alert and pray. Otherwise temptation will overpower you. For the spirit indeed is willing, but how weak the body is! (Matthew 26:41, TLB*)*

June 8, 1994, is a day I'll never forget. After serving four years and six months of my ten-year sentence, I was released early for good behavior from the Kettle Moraine Correctional Facility. It was a warm, sunny June day. The inmates and guards gave me a great deal of support. I'd been a model prisoner.

Before my release, staff members and inmates encouraged me to stay clean. They gave me the same advice over and over: Don't follow the same pattern; do some volunteer work; learn some skills; be a good father and a law-abiding citizen; get a job; stay home; go to church; and if you do go someplace, tell someone where you're going.

I told the prison officials that I'd be moving back in with my old girlfriend, Janice, the mother of one of my three children. I also said I believed I would find work quickly in Milwaukee because I'd lived there and had a number of contacts.

My actual release date was suppose to be in September 1996. I believed it was God's intervention for me to be released two-and-a-half years early. I thought of Jeff. I was still sad for him, sad that he would live in prison for the rest of his life. I never stopped praying for him.

I left Kettle Moraine at 8 a.m. An officer took me and some other inmates to the bus stop where we boarded the bus to Milwaukee. The clothing I wore came from the Salvation Army–used clothing, but much better than the prison clothing I'd been wearing for more than four years. It reminded me of growing up, but this time I was grateful for those hand-me-down clothes.

I knew my life wasn't going to be easy and I was a little afraid. I knew that sometimes men who were in prison had a difficult time adjusting to life outside of prison. It can be hard to get back on their feet and sometimes they pick up right where they left off because that's all they know. I wasn't sure what to expect, but I knew what I wanted and I knew I didn't want to go back to prison.

The first thing I did when I got to Milwaukee was make a beeline to Janice's house. That was a big mistake. She had a new boyfriend and they didn't want anything to do with me. She wouldn't even let me see my son, mainly because she and her new boyfriend were on drugs and she was pretty spaced out.

I needed to get away from there. If I associated with anyone doing drugs while I was on parole, I could be sent back to prison. I left with just two hundred dollars in my pocket, no place to stay, no job, and no prospects.

I called Nancy and Jerry Christianson. Jerry was in prison many years ago, but God saved him, and now he and his wife run New Song Ministries. They picked me up and took me to meet Vern, a friend of theirs in West Allis who was also involved in New Song Ministries.

There were six of us at Vern's place. We prayed, praised God, and sang songs. The whole time I felt that the devil was still trying to tempt me, saying, "you've been gone too long and I know you want to get back into the mess of things."

I couldn't sit still. I kept getting up, trying to find excuses not to sing. I'd go out for a cigarette. Then I'd come back in and sit down. Then I'd get up again. I just wasn't ready for all this singing and praising God. I needed to do something.

When I looked back on that afternoon, I realized the devil was having a heyday with me. All afternoon I was up and down, up and down thinking, wanting to go, but not knowing where.

The devil worked hard inside me. I prayed, asking God to help me relax. I knew that God had sent me Jerry and Nancy and I needed to put my faith in what God had in mind for me.

Trouble was, I was scared that before long I'd be doing some of the things I did before. Finally, I gave in to the devil, left Vern's place, and went back to my old girlfriend's apartment to pick up some clothes I'd left there before I went to prison.

My Release from Prison

She kicked me out and told me I couldn't ever stay there again. She shut the door on me. I decided to go to the Salvation Army and ask for help.

I got into a cab but, on the way, asked the cab driver to stop when I saw a woman walking on the street near 20th and Lisbon. I knew prostitutes frequented that neighborhood. That woman was one and I stayed with her that night.

The next morning I felt terrible. I was upset with myself for giving in to the devil and hooking up with that prostitute, and because my old girlfriend was with another man. I thought I still loved her.

One thing's for sure, I still had all my same old problems. No money, no job, no prospects, and here I was sinning again.

That afternoon I went to the Milwaukee Rescue Mission and called Jerry and Nancy again. They were supportive. They picked me up and prayed for me. They got me a room at the Philadelphia Church of God in Christ on North Martin Luther King Drive.

Pastor Barden ministers to prisoners and he let me stay in the Brotherhood House over the church. When you stayed there, the pastor expected you to attend Pentecostal church services three days a week, including Bible study. I stayed for a short time while I worked a few temporary jobs.

All the while, I thought about my kids and my old girlfriends. A lot of my previous sins and crimes came into my head. The devil worked me over pretty good in those days, but because I followed the Brotherhood House rules, I stayed out of trouble.

One day I met another brother who belonged to Parklawn Assembly of God church. He invited me to meet Pastor Harvey and to attend services there. I met a woman on the bus who was also on her way to Parklawn. We talked about Christ and got to know each other a little more whenever we saw each other at services.

One night the woman called me and said she was lonely. I knew if I left the Brotherhood House and spent the night with her, I'd break curfew and get kicked out… but I did it anyway. Why, I kept wondering, is the flesh so weak?

It was a big mistake. It added nothing but chaos to my life. She was a married woman, separated but not divorced. One day the pastor's sermon

137

discussed the immorality of being unfaithful to a spouse and the sinfulness of trying to covet thy neighbor's wife. It seemed like he and everyone in the church was talking directly to me. I finally told the pastor about the woman but he said he already knew.

I got a room elsewhere and worked various temporary jobs. I eventually went back to the woman's house because every other place I ended up was nothing but a drug house. People dealt and took drugs all around me, and I couldn't risk being caught with folks like that.

By the second week in November 1994, I knew I needed to leave Milwaukee altogether. I called my sister and brother in St. Louis and asked them to come and get me. For a fleeting moment, I missed prison and I understood why some people wanted to go back. In prison you don't have to worry about women, money, finding a place to sleep, or finding a job. In prison there also isn't the everyday struggle of trying to stay clean from drugs and alcohol. There is a lot less temptation in prison.

I thought about Jeff and wondered how he was doing. I hadn't written a letter to him since my release. I heard about him in the news occasionally. Both his parents had been in the media, discussing their roles in Jeff's life. His father, Lionel was writing a biography on Jeff and their family life. Jeff had said to me once during our time together that someday the world would be writing books about him—I guess he was right.

His mother, Joyce, also had been in the news a few times and talked about how she loved Jeff even though he did terrible things.

Apparently both his parents visited him in prison. In some ways I was jealous of Jeff, having parents who loved him regardless of his wrongs. He had people there for him, who supported him; he even had priests and people like me who wrote him letters about staying with God. I needed that kind of support. I started to think that maybe I needed a letter telling me about God, love, and strength more than he did right now. I felt lost.

My family picked me up and I moved to Florissant, Missouri, a St. Louis suburb where my sister lived.

My Release from Prison

Four days after Thanksgiving, on November 28, 1994, I received a shocking call from an old Milwaukee friend.

"Calvin, did you hear that Dahmer's dead?"

I couldn't believe what I was hearing. My friend told me that I needed to come to Milwaukee because reporters wanted to interview me. I wasn't sure whether I wanted to talk about Jeff right then but, at the same time, I knew there was a side to Jeff that no one else saw or understood. A lot of people, *most* people, called him a monster. However, I believed there really was a good side to Jeff, one that the world needed to see.

I boarded a plane that night and flew back to Milwaukee. I read the Chicago papers during a layover.

That's when it hit me.

Jeffrey Dahmer was dead.

His search for peace and understanding of the Lord's forgiveness was over. I was sad as I read those newspapers in Chicago.

As soon as I got to Milwaukee, I caught pneumonia and was admitted to St. Joseph's Hospital. Reporters from Channel 12-TV interviewed me, but the interviews weren't good because I was too sick.

Jeff's death struck me to the core. It hurt to think that he was gone. I felt sorry for him and I felt bad, partly because of the way he died. He had already suffered so much in prison, but I told myself that God looked out for him.

I knew Jeff had requested and been baptized in May 1994 by a Church of Christ minister named Roy Ratcliff from Madison. Jeff wore a white robe and Radcliff submerged him in the prison's steel whirlpool normally used for handicapped inmates.

I was so happy Jeff was baptized. He finally let Jesus into his heart. During an interview, Ratcliff said that Jeff was completely sincere and wanted to live a new life. He wasn't baptized for selfish reasons; Jeff did it because he wanted to be with God and looked forward to a life and an afterlife with God. Jeff finally let go of his demons.

For me personally, I knew in my heart that God forgave Dahmer's sins.

That gave me some peace of mind during the next days. I felt relief knowing that our time together had helped him, in some form, to realize God's goodness and helped him to see that even a serial killer's soul could be saved.

Twenty-Four
The Murder of Jeffrey Dahmer

For the time has come for judgment, and it must begin first among God's own children. And if even we who are Christians must be judged, what terrible fate awaits those who have never believed in the Lord? (I Peter 4:17, TLB)

November 28, 1994.

The headline of the *Milwaukee Journal* blared across the page in thick, black letters: "Dahmer Slain in Prison." Jeffrey Dahmer had served a little more than two years and nine months of his sixteen consecutive life sentences.

When he was brutally murdered in the bathroom near the prison gymnasium on that gray November day, Jeffrey was thirty-four years old. That morning he ate breakfast with the other prisoners in his unit. At 7:50 a.m., officers escorted Jeff from his cell to his job cleaning the gym. Just twenty minutes later, security found Jeff and another white prisoner, Jesse Anderson, both in pools of blood with multiple skull fractures, both men savagely beaten.

An ambulance sped Dahmer to Divine Savior Hospital in Portage, just a few miles from the prison. At 9:11 a.m., just an hour after he was beaten, Dahmer was pronounced dead from massive head injuries.

Anderson died two days later from his injuries.

Later another prisoner, twenty-five year old Christopher J. Scarver, confessed. He worked with the two inmates, cleaning the prison gym bathroom. He used a twenty-inch metal bar he had removed from a piece of exercise equipment in the gym to bash Dahmer's head during the attack.

Scarver was a convicted murderer serving a life sentence at Columbia for the 1990 execution-style shooting death of Steven J. Lohman. Lohman had worked with Scarver at the Wisconsin Conservation Corps. Even before he murdered Dahmer, Scarver would not have been eligible for parole until 2042.

After Dahmer's death, people asked why Jeffrey had been alone and unsupervised in the prison bathroom. Officers at Columbia said Dahmer could have asked for a more segregated, more secure living and working arrangement, but he chose to be out with the general prison population. I heard that, because it was during the holidays, the prison guards were more relaxed. The guards thought since nothing had happened in the past so nothing would happen then. Scarver and Dahmer were unsupervised for a little more than twenty minutes.

The night of Jeff's death, as I was on my way to Milwaukee, I watched the news on TV and I read the coverage in the newspapers. Some people said it was tragic that Dahmer was dead because now he couldn't assist medical science by telling them what made him do the things he did. They believed that because he was an intelligent, articulate man, he could have helped society deal with or perhaps prevent other potential serial killers from murdering.

In St. Louis, Chicago, and Milwaukee, I heard people talking about Scarver's motive for killing Dahmer. Were his actions racially motivated? Was Scarver angry with whites in general? Various media reports over the next few months said Scarver had depression, psychosis, delusions, bi-polar disorder, manic depression, and schizophrenia, and took anti-psychotic medications. Scarver claimed to hear voices that would tell him what to do, say, and whom to trust. He said those voices told him that he was the Son of God, the "chosen one," and that he was suppose to kill Dahmer. Scarver apparently planned the murder.

Scarver entered a plea of not guilty due to mental illness during his trial for the murders of Dahmer and Anderson. However, the judge ruled Scarver was mentally competent to stand trial. Scarver was charged with both murders and received two more life sentences in addition to his current life sentence for Lohman's murder.

I found out that a year or so after Scarver's conviction, he was transferred to the federal prison in Florence, Colorado, known to be one of the most secure prisons in the U.S. federal system. The Wisconsin prison system thought he was too dangerous and feared for the safety of the guards and inmates.

Scarver eventually returned to Wisconsin to the Supermax prison in Boscobel, the state's most secure maximum-security prison, where he continues to serve his time.

During the week after Jeffrey's death, the media interviewed many family members of Dahmer's victims. Few expressed sadness over his death; most were glad he was gone.

The general lack of remorse over Dahmer's death was understandable. And, although few people actually mourned his passing, I was among those who did grieve. I remembered all the late-night talks I had with him from our adjoining cells at Columbia. I remembered his anguished, twisted feelings about his victims and the way he carried out the murders. I recalled the many conversations we'd had about Jesus Christ and the lessons for living a good life that Jesus had left for us in the New Testament.

I thought about all the letters I'd written to Jeff, the ones written when we were both at Columbia and the dozens of letters I wrote to him after I was moved from the cell next to him, to Racine, and finally to Kettle Moraine.

Since March 1992, I'd tried so hard to share with Jeff the goodness of the Lord in those letters that when he was murdered, I truly felt emptiness inside me. I wondered if Jeff was at peace. Had my messages gotten through to him? Had he truly accepted Jesus Christ as his Lord and Savior? Did Jeff really believe that Jesus died for his sins, the most brutal, vicious sins imaginable? I wondered and thought and prayed.

That night I opened my Bible to II Timothy.

I have fought long and hard for my Lord, and through it all I have kept true to him. And now the time has come for me to stop fighting and rest. In heaven a crown is waiting for me which the Lord, the righteous Judge, will give me on that great day of his return. And not just to me, but to all those whose lives show that they are eagerly looking forward to his coming back again. (II Timothy 4:7-8, *TLB*)

Was Jeffrey Dahmer now at total rest and peace with God in heaven? I remembered the many times I'd read Jeffrey the comforting words in Ephesians.

Stop being mean, bad-tempered and angry. Quarreling, harsh words, and dislike of others should have no place in your lives. Instead, be kind to each other, tender-hearted, forgiving one another, just as God has forgiven you because you belong to Christ. (Ephesians 4:31-32, *TLB*)

After I'd read those words to Jeffrey, I'd say, "Jeff, it doesn't matter what you've done, if you repent sincerely, God will forgive you. He will forgive anyone for anything, many, many times. He has forgiven me so many times. Alleluia, thank you, God!"

I recalled another of what seemed like Jeffrey's favorite verses from Mark.

But when you are praying, first forgive anyone you are holding a grudge against, so that your Father in heaven will forgive you your sins too. (Mark 11:25, *TLB*)

It seemed Dahmer had slowly but surely come to grips with the knowledge that even *his* sins could be forgiven.

I remember he told me once he especially liked the way Psalms 102 began: "Lord, hear my prayer! Listen to my plea!" Jeff liked that verse because he, too, was crying out. He was tired and wanted forgiveness.

I hoped that I helped to show Jeff the way. I believe I gave him the tools. With the help from other ministers, priests, nuns, and his baptism, Jeff had everything he needed.

I don't think Jeff ever thought about God and forgiveness until he got to prison. That's why prison was the best thing that ever happened to him. Prison gave him the opportunity to be with people filled with God's forgiving spirit.

Jeffrey Dahmer did horrible things and hurt many people. He suffered a lifelong battle with Satan. I'm sure it is easy for people who did not experience what I had experienced to doubt Dahmer's sincerity. Only after his arrest did he begin to have an interest in faith. This leaves us with many questions. Was Jeff's decision to be baptized and learn about God all for selfish, earthly motives? Was he just doing it to have people take pity on him, with hopes of getting a lighter jail sentence down the road? Was he like the hypocrites Jesus talked about in the Bible, people who act holy to get good graces but in reality have hearts of stone? Or was Jeff truly sorry for the wrongs he committed and wanted to live a new life with God?

Everyone must draw their own conclusions about Dahmer's sincerity and decide for himself or herself what was really in his or her heart.

But the most important spiritual question will always remain: Did God forgive Jeffrey Dahmer for his horrible sins against humanity?

Truly, only God can answer that question.

I believe with all my heart that as long as Jeffrey didn't blaspheme our Lord Jesus Christ, and if he truly asked for it, he certainly received the gift of forgiveness. I believe he was earnestly seeking God and wasn't putting on a show for sympathy. As time went on, both while I was with him and in the next couple of years when I saw him on TV, it was evident to me by his voice, facial expressions, and the things he said that he seemed truly sorry for his sins. Jeff apologized to the ones he hurt and said he wished he had never done the things he did.

Furthermore, he wanted to learn about God. He wanted to learn about a life not shrouded by Satan's darkness but filled with the forgiving truth and light of God. It is my conviction that in the end the truth really did set Jeffrey free. Just as it will for all of us, if we only believe.

Today you will be with me in Paradise. This is a solemn promise. (Luke 23:43, *TLB*)

Take Care – Jeff

Afterword

If you only knew what a wonderful gift God has for you, and who I am,
*you would ask me for some living water! (John 4:10, **TLB**)*

My experience with Jeffrey Dahmer was both frightening and enlightening. He was, for many, the scariest, most evil man on earth. I heard in the media that even after he died and was taken to the morgue at the University of Wisconsin hospital in Madison, his feet remained shackled.

I also read that doctors removed Dahmer's brain, preserving it for future study. Jeff's mother, Joyce, wanted his brain studied to see if there was some biological physical evidence for why this happened to her son.

According to his will, Jeff wanted his body cremated as soon as possible and he didn't want a funeral service. Officials preserved his body until after the trial of his killer, Christopher Scarver, then it was cremated.

Lionel Dahmer wanted Jeff's brain cremated, too, against the wishes of his ex-wife. Lionel insisted there was nothing to learn from Jeff's brain and that it was time to let go of the past. The two went to court and a judge ruled in favor of Lionel. Jeff's brain was cremated on December 12, 1995. Lionel and Joyce split Jeff's ashes and both tried to move on and live normal lives.

In 1996, an independent third party bought Dahmer's belongings and destroyed them out of state so no one could ever find them.

If Jeff were still alive, he would be continuing to serve his life sentences. If he were still alive, I know I would still be writing to him and praying for him. I would still be telling him not to give up, and to put his life in God's hands.

Even now, even after all these years, I still think about Jeff. It's comforting for me to believe that he is finally at peace with himself, his crimes, men like Scarver who wronged him, and is with God in heaven.

I have told you my story with the hope that it may make you think about the power of God's forgiveness. I give my highest thanks to God, who assisted with this project. I also thank God for all the messages about his goodness that are there for all of us in the Holy Bible, messages that have helped me learn what it means to be a Christian.

When we walk with God, we walk with a new assurance. Our problems may stay, our circumstances may not change, but we must know that God is in control. We, as Christians, must focus on God's adequacy, not on our own inadequacies.

Because of my experience with Jeffrey Dahmer, I learned that there is no end to the seasons of fresh encounters we may have with God. We can never exhaust his goodness. Each time we have a personal encounter with Him, we will see more clearly our own weaknesses and that will help us, in turn, magnify the awesome reality of Christ's love for us.

I also believe that God put a new being in Jeff's heart. God called him to serve in all ways. It says in Deuteronomy 4:29 that "you shall find him when you search for him with all your hearts and souls." II Corinthians 5:17 also tells us that when you accept Jesus Christ as your personal Lord and Savior, "he becomes a brand new person inside. He is not the same any more. A new life has begun!" (*TLB*)

I believe Jeffrey accepted Christ as his Savior and at that moment he, too, became new. His sins were forgiven and, from that moment, God never gave up on him.

Many people believe that God can only forgive sins that are no worse than the ones they, themselves commit. They think that God won't or can't possibly forgive sins against humanity such as the ones Dahmer committed. I say to those people to read Matthew 17:20: "For if you had faith even as small as a tiny mustard seed you could say to this mountain, 'Move!' and it would go far away. Nothing would be impossible." (*TLB*)

As Christians we must believe that nothing is impossible for God, including forgiveness of sins we think are beyond forgiveness.

I believe that, during the last years of his life, Jeffrey Dahmer took comfort in knowing God, his son Jesus Christ and the Holy Spirit. After all, God

AFTERWORD

did make a promise to us that if we serve with all our hearts, he will restore what the devil has destroyed within us. That promise is in John 3:3, "Unless you are born again, you can never get into the Kingdom of God." (*TLB*)

When asked what "born again" meant, Jesus answered in John 3:5, "What I am telling you so earnestly is this: Unless one is born of water and the Spirit, he cannot enter the Kingdom of God." (*TLB*) In other words, we must be baptized into the Christian faith.

During his incarceration at Columbia, in spring 1994, Jeffrey was baptized in a ceremony that guaranteed his entrance into the Kingdom of God. At that moment he was no longer an evil man possessed by the devil, but rather, a new creation.

The promise is there in John 5:24. Jesus himself was talking. "I say emphatically that anyone who listens to my message and believes in God who sent me has eternal life, and will never be damned for his sins, but has already passed out of death into life." (*TLB*)

My prayer for each person who reads this book is that you have already or will soon experience the same goodness, forgiveness, and power of God, the Holy Spirit, and our Lord Jesus Christ, that Jeffrey Dahmer experienced. I also pray that you, too, will have the profound experience of sharing your faith with another lost soul the way I did.

God bless you.

Herman Martin

FINAL NOTES
∞

During the process of researching and writing this book, based on the notes Herman Martin kept in prison, I interviewed many people including Dick Heath, special investigator for Milwaukee's district attorney. Heath was present and videotaped the four-day, twenty-four-hour interview that prosecuting psychiatrist Dr. Park Dietz conducted with Jeffrey Dahmer before the trial.

During that time, while Heath listened as Dahmer carefully detailed his crimes for Dr. Dietz, Heath indicated he never once saw or heard any racial motivation for what Dahmer did, nor did he hear any indication of racial prejudice from the prisoner himself.

Heath told me, "Jeffrey Dahmer did not brag or boast about his crimes in any way during any of the interviews I observed. Dahmer's victims were white, black, Asian, American Indian, Hispanic, and Puerto Rican. The race didn't matter to him. In fact, Jeff was kind to minorities. What he wanted was a young, small-boned, smooth-skinned male with a good physique. Jeff Dahmer was not a violent man. He never took one victim to his apartment against his will. He drugged all his victims before he killed them. It's true, he was a coward who avoided confrontation, but he was definitely not a racist."

While I wrote this book and read Herman's notes that repeated over and over his belief that Dahmer was a racist, I asked Herman, "How could Dahmer say those hateful things about blacks when you, his friend, are a black man? How could the special investigator who witnessed twenty-four hours of questioning of Dahmer by Dr. Dietz, say that Jeff definitely was not a racist?"

Herman responded, "Mr. Heath was not in prison with the man. He's entitled to his opinion. When I was in prison, I told doctors what I thought they wanted to hear. All prisoners do that. I think this is what Dahmer did, but he didn't tell them everything. He was a racist. A prisoner will tell another prisoner the true story and based on what Jeff Dahmer told me in prison, I'd say he was a racist."

Like Herman says in the last chapter, "Only God knows for sure."

I just wanted to share both sides of the story.

Patricia Lorenz

ABOUT THE AUTHORS

Herman Martin struggles daily to get back on his feet and stay with God because life outside prison is full of temptations. He has fought to gain control of his life by addressing his drug addiction. With the help of rehabilitation treatment centers in Milwaukee, he has tried hard to stay clean and avoid risky behaviors and situations. He has been to many centers, for both himself and for loved ones also struggling with addictions. The centers have helped by providing Herman with support, guidance, and the tools he needs to be successful in staying focused and taking responsibility for himself and for his drug recovery.

Herman plans to use the profits from this book to help his family as partial repayment for what he has taken from them and for all the pain he has caused. He also wants to give back to the community, helping those who are struggling with addictions and homelessness. He wants to make a difference.

Patricia Lorenz is an art-of-living writer and speaker. She's the author of a dozen books and hundreds of articles and stories in magazines and newspapers. She lived in Milwaukee for twenty-four years, including the years Jeffrey Dahmer was committing his crimes. She also worked at Milwaukee's radio station, WTMJ, during the time that station broadcast the entire Dahmer trial.